GETTING TO KNOW
CUBA

A TRAVEL GUIDE

Hot

by Jane McManus

St. Martin's Press, New York

First Edition
10 9 8 7 6 5 4 3 2 1

Photos by Gustavo Maynulet, Tony Lorenzo and Author

Maps by Vantage Art based on those published by the Cuban Geodesy and Cartography Institute (ICGC) and design by Janet Koenig

Cover art: *Vuelta a Cuba* (Trip through Cuba) by Cuban ceramicist, José Rodríguez Fúster.

PRODUCTION TEAM:

Robert Bedell, Production Coordinator
Janet Koenig, Art Director and Editorial Consultant
Your Type, Typesetter
Rina Benmayor, Proofreader
James O'Brien, Indexer
South Sea International Press Ltd., Printer

_ONTENTS

PRACTICAL INFORMATION   *I*

TRAVELING TO CUBA   1
  US Travel Ban   1
  Airline Connections   2
  Travel Documents   2
  Time   3
  Customs Regulations   3
  Health Regulations   3
  When to Go   3
  What to Pack   4
  Money   4
  Travel to Third Countries   5
  Cuban Tourism Promotion Offices   7

TRAVELING IN CUBA   9
  Flora and Fauna   9
  By Road   11
  Maps and Addresses   13
  Planes, Boats and Trains   13
  Communications   14
  Accommodations   15
  Meals   16
  In Case of Illness   16

GETTING TO KNOW CUBA THROUGH ITS HISTORY   *17*

CONQUISTADORES, INDIANS AND SLAVES   17
PIRATES, SMUGGLERS AND *VEGUEROS*   19
AFTER THE BRITISH, THINGS WERE NEVER THE SAME   20
SUGAR, SLAVES AND REBELLION   21
CUBA'S TEN YEARS' WAR OF INDEPENDENCE (1868-1878)   23
THE NECESSARY WAR (1895)   26
US INTERVENTION (1898) AND MANIPULATION   28
CRISIS, DICTATORSHIP AND REVOLUTION   31

A NEW ERA   35
  Blockade and Harassment   36
  Defense and Organizations   37
  Party and Government   38
  The Economy   38
  The Fabric of Life   39
  Sports and Culture   40
  The Cuban People   43

GETTING TO KNOW CUBA BY SEEING IT   45

HAVANA   **45**
  OLD HAVANA   45
    Arms Square   49
    Off Arms Square   52
    Old Square   55
    Cathedral Square   56
    Presidential Palace and Angel Hill   60
    Museum of Fine Arts   63
    Near Central Park   63
    Prado Promenade   64
    Morro Castle and La Punta   67
    Across the Bay   68

  NEW HAVANA   69
    Along the Malecón   69
    La Rampa   70
    Tropicana Nightclub   71
    From La Rampa   73
    To Revolution Square   73
    Paseo to the Sea   75
    Miramar   76
    On the Outskirts   78
    To Lenin Park   80
    Where Hemingway Lived   82
    From Africa to the Arabian Nights   82
    East Havana Beaches   83

PINAR DEL RIO PROVINCE   **86**
SOROA   86
MASPOTON   88
SAN DIEGO DE LOS BAÑOS   88
LA GÜIRA NATIONAL PARK   88
PINAR DEL RIO   89
VIÑALES VALLEY   90
VUELTA ABAJO   91

THE ISLE OF YOUTH   **92**
A HISTORY OF PLUNDER   93
TODAY'S WEALTH   95

CAYO LARGO   **97**

MATANZAS PROVINCE   **98**
VARADERO BEACH   98
Where to Eat   100
As for Music   103
MATANZAS   104
CARDENAS   106
THE ZAPATA PENINSULA   107

VILLA CLARA PROVINCE   **109**
SANTA CLARA   109
REMEDIOS   111
Around the Square   112
Las Parrandas   114
CAIBARIEN AND CAYO CONUCO   115
ELGUEA BATHS   116
LAKE HANABANILLA   116

CIENFUEGOS PROVINCE   **118**
CIENFUEGOS   118
Downtown   119
On the Outskirts   120

SANCTI SPIRITUS PROVINCE   **121**
TRINIDAD   121
Sugar and Slavery   121

Trinitarian Traditions 124
Sugarmill Valley 125
SANCTI SPIRITUS 126

CIEGO DE AVILA PROVINCE 127
CIEGO DE AVILA 127
MORON 127
CAYO GUILLERMO 128

CAMAGÜEY PROVINCE 129
CAMAGÜEY 129
SANTA LUCIA BEACH 132
GUAIMARO 133

HOLGUIN PROVINCE 134
HOLGUIN 134
Colonial Center 134
Modern Rim 136
Mayabe Lookout 136
BARIAY NATIONAL PARK 137
GUARDALAVACA BEACH 137
GIBARA 138
BARIAY BEACH 138
BANES 138

GRANMA PROVINCE 140
BAYAMO 140
MANZANILLO 142
LA DEMAJAGUA 142
MEDIA LUNA 143
LAS COLORADAS BEACH 143
MAREA DEL PORTILLO BEACH 144
SIERRA MAESTRA NATIONAL PARK 145

SANTIAGO DE CUBA PROVINCE 146
SANTIAGO DE CUBA 146
Moncada 146
Céspedes Park 148
Cultural Feast 149
Santiago Carnival 151

Taking It All In	152
The Morro of Santiago	153
Cayo Granma	155
DOS RIOS	156
EL COBRE	156
Miracles	156
Rebellion	157
The Virgin and the Basilica	158
BACONAO PARK	159
San Juan Hill	159
Gran Piedra	160
Granjita Siboney	160
Along the Coast	160
GUANTANAMO PROVINCE	**162**
GUANTANAMO	162
BARACOA	162
The Fortresses	163
The Malecón	165
The Flavor of Baracoa	165
SPECIALIZED TOURISM	**167**
CONVENTIONS	167
FESTIVALS	167
HEALTH	169
SPORTS	170
Bird Watching	170
Fishing	170
Hunting	171
Scuba Diving	172
STUDY	172
GETTING TO KNOW CUBA IN SPANISH	*175*
TEN MINICONVERSATIONS	175
1. Greetings and Introductions	175
2. Money and Shopping	176
3. Catching the Bus	177

4.	Driving	178
5.	Taking Pictures	178
6.	Problems	179
7.	Sports and Recreation	179
8.	In Case of Illness	180
9.	Night Life	180
10.	Wining and Dining	181

EATING VOCABULARY   182
GLOSSARY OF USEFUL WORDS AND PHRASES   183
    Days of the Week   183
    Months of the Year   183
    Time, Distance, Numbers   184
    In the Hotel   185
    Telephone Calls   187

INDEX   189

MAPS:
    Cuba Provinces   10
    Havana   46
    Varadero   98
    Trinidad   122
    Santiago de Cuba   147

ACKNOWLEDGEMENTS

Many people helped with this guide, first and foremost my colleagues at PUBLICITUR: General Director Gary González, who approved the idea; EDITUR Editor-in-Chief Raquel Saavedra, who read the manuscript and made valuable criticisms and suggestions; and all the writers and artists who shared information and ideas. I am also grateful to the many provincial tourism officials who went out of their way to be helpful. Havana historian Eusebio Leal's office provided access to documents and cleared up many doubts. And special thanks go to Inés Girona of Cuba's National Institute of Tourism (INTUR) for her meticulous and knowledgeable copy reading of the text.

The guide in its present form could never have been finished without the help and interest of English-speaking friends and relatives. Most especially I thank my ever-encouraging and supportive husband Bill Brent; friends Rina Benmayor, Darlene Korab, Mary Todd and Marge Zimmerman, whose knowledge of Cuba, Cuban Spanish and English proved invaluable; Margery Moore, who generously gave me her notes for a travel guide on Cuba; Jack Speyer, who ferreted out literary references and old guides to Cuba; Bill Price, whose interest in US-Cuba connections fed mine; my two enthusiastic and talented editors in the United States: the late Madelon Berns Bedell and Sharon Mayberry, whose perceptive — and often coinciding — comments led to major revisions; Peggy Gilpin, my invaluable consultant on the final manuscript; group leaders Betty and Herman Liveright, who read it with all the awareness of what visitors want to know about Cuba; my niece Jane Bedell, who tested the manuscript and found it practical; and my brother Robert Bedell, who coordinated printing, contacts and deliveries .

The guide might never have gotten beyond a computer printout without the perseverence of Frances Goldin, literary agent and friend, who always shared my conviction that thousands of people really are interested in *Getting to Know Cuba*.

INTRODUCTION

This guide is for you, the curious traveler, who wants to touch and smell and feel the differences and similarities between home and the place you're visiting; who goes to a foreign country with the hope of seeing new things, meeting people of another culture and learning something about how they live, how they see things, where they're coming from. As a curious traveler you like to get out on the streets, wander around, experience and communicate — in the belief that a good vacation offers both change and exchange.

Certainly the color, form, motion, temperature, taste, texture and sound of Havana or Santiago de Cuba will be a change from any English-speaking city; and the friendly, outgoing Cuban people — whether or not they speak English — will do everything possible to exchange information with you. Of course, they'll love it if you're able to say a few phrases in Spanish.

Cuba is a bright, sometimes bewildering, kaleidoscope. Hopefully, *Getting to Know Cuba* will help you focus and interpret what you see, hear and experience on this endlessly fascinating island.

PRACTICAL INFORMATION

TRAVELING TO CUBA

Trips to Cuba on regularly scheduled or charter flights can be arranged through any tour operator or travel agent that does business with Cuba. For general information, contact any of the Cuban tourism promotion offices listed at the end of this section.

US Travel Ban

The current US ban on travel to Cuba — actually a series of Treasury Department regulations that prohibit citizens from spending money in Cuba — has been extremely successful in preventing US tourists from visiting the most interesting island in the Caribbean, at the same time that thousands of unrestricted Canadian neighbors spend both time and money there and seem to love it.

Exempt from the US travel ban are journalists, certain graduate degree candidates, professionals doing full-time research in their fields with an established interest in Cuba, people with family in Cuba and anyone invited by Cuba with all land expenses paid. These people qualify under the "general license" to travel to and spend money in Cuba without asking permission from the Treasury Department, although the carrier usually asks them to sign a form certifying they qualify and under what provision. Anyone else must request an individual license from the Treasury Deparment.

Travelers from the US need a visa to enter Cuba, which is arranged through the travel agent or the Cuban Interests Section in Washington, D.C.

Marazul Tours, Inc., 250 West 57th Street, Suite 1311, New York, N.Y. 10107; tel.: (212) 582-9570 in New York and (800) 223-5334 outside New York State; telex: 220712, is the travel agency in the United States that books trips to Cuba.

Airline Connections

Cubana de Aviación has regularly scheduled flights between Cuba and Angola, Argentina, Barbados, Belgium, Canada, Czechoslovakia, France, the German Democratic Republic, Guyana, Jamaica, Mexico, Nicaragua, Panama, Peru, Spain and Trinidad and Tobago. Regular charter flights connect Cuba with Argentina, Austria, Brazil, Canada, the Federal Republic of Germany, Italy and the United States.

Foreign airlines with offices in Havana include: Aeroflot, Air Canada, Air France, CSA, Iberia, Interflug, KLM, Mexicana, Sabena and several charter companies. Travel from the United States is via Miami-Havana charter, Cubana's and Air Canada's regularly scheduled flights from Montreal and Toronto, or Cubana and Mexicana from Mexico City.

Travel Documents

Visitors flying to Cuba must present a valid passport and visa or tourist card on entering the country unless they are in transit. In that case, they may remain in Cuba for 72 hours without such documents and may leave the airport provided they have confirmed reservations for an ongoing flight.

Entrance procedures for cruise ship passengers are fulfilled by presentation of the passenger list to Cuban immigration officials. Main points of entry are Havana and Santiago de Cuba.

Yachtsmen must request permission of CUBATUR at least 20 days prior to the expected date of arrival at Havana's Hemingway Marina, Varadero, Santiago de Cuba or Cienfuegos, giving the following information: type of vessel and number of masts, name, color, length, draught, registration, flag, port of origin, port of arrival, approximate date of arrival and the names and passport numbers of all those who will be aboard.

Pilots of private planes must notify Havana's Civil Aeronautics Flight Control Office 72 hours before departure, specifying point of departure, destination, date and estimated time of arrival in Cuba and purpose of trip as well as plane ownership, type and classification, color, registration and number and the names and passport numbers of those aboard.

Time

Cuba is on Eastern Standard Time (Daylight Saving in summer) like the east coast of North America. When it's noon in Havana, it's 6 p.m. in London.

Customs Regulations

Visitors intending to spend more than 24 hours and less than six months in Cuba are considered tourists and may bring in, duty-free, personal effects, camera (German, Japanese and Kodak film can be purchased in Cuba, but color Kodak cannot be developed locally), tape recorder, record player, typewriter, portable TV and camping and sports equipment (including hunting rifle). These items should be listed on the customs declaration and must be taken home with you.

Firearms, drugs, medicine other than that prescribed for personal use and pornographic materials are specifically banned.

Health Regulations

No health certificate is required of visitors arriving from countries that, like Cuba, are free of the diseases registered in international health regulations. Travelers arriving from areas where cholera, smallpox or yellow fever exist must present a certificate of vaccination against those diseases.

Animals, animal products and plants must be surrendered to Cuban health authorities for determination of quarantine, admission or nonadmission measures.

When to Go

Visitors from northern climes usually prefer the warm tropical winter — the mean temperature in January-February,

Cuba's coldest months, is 22° C. (71.3° F.) — to the scorching summer — mean July-August temperature is 29° C. (84.1° F.) and that is also when most Cubans are on vacation so that beaches, hotels and restaurants are more crowded.

If your vacation happens to coincide with a national holiday, festivities may outweigh the fact that most offices, museums and schools are closed. Cuba has four such holidays: January 1, the Day of National Liberation, marks the triumph of the Cuban Revolution in 1959; May Day is celebrated with workers' parades; July 26, Day of National Rebellion (which includes July 25 and 27), the date Fidel Castro and his followers attacked the Moncada Garrison in 1953, is recognized as the start of the Revolution; and October 10 commemorates the declaration of the War of Independence against Spain in 1868.

What to Pack

Cool casual cottons are essential for comfort in a tropical climate where the humidity hovers around 80 percent, making it seem hotter than the thermometer indicates. Include a stole, sweater or lightweight jacket for a cool evening and the frigid air-conditioning you're apt to encounter in theaters, restaurants and other public buildings. Electric current is 110 volts, 60 cycles, and appliances should have flat-pronged plugs. Although toiletries are available in the hotel stores, you may not find the item or brand name you're looking for so it's best to bring your own, including a good sunscreen. Sun glasses and comfortable walking shoes are musts. No need to pack last year's straw hat since you'll surely want a Cuban *sombrero*. And don't forget your bathing suit.

Money

The Cuban monetary unit is the peso, composed of 100 centavos. Coins of one, two, five, 20 and 40 centavos and a peso and bills of one, three, five, ten and 20 pesos are in general circulation. Visitors are advised to exchange only small amounts of their own currency into Cuban pesos, since the legal exchange rate is generally unfavorable and pesos are not accepted in the tourism network.

Visitors to Cuba can pay for goods and services in most foreign currencies, traveler's checks or the Exchange Certificates issued by the National Bank of Cuba. These certificates are equal in value to the US dollar and may be purchased with any other foreign currency. Prices are listed in US dollars in tourist installations, but the equivalent amount may also be paid directly in the following currencies: Austrian schilling, Belgian franc, British pound sterling, Canadian dollar, Danish krone, Dutch gulden, Finnish markka, French franc, German deutsche mark, Italian lira, Japanese yen, Mexican peso, Norwegian krone, Portuguese escudo, Spanish peseta, Swedish krona, Swiss franc and Venezuelan bolívar.

Currency can be exchanged at the hotel front desk or at any branch of the National Bank of Cuba. On departure from Cuba, up to 10 pesos and all unused Exchange Certificates can be reexchanged.

Access, Diners Club, Eurocard, MasterCard and Visa credit cards issued outside the United States are accepted in tourist hotels and restaurants.

Travel to Third Countries

Extensions of visas and visas to third countries are arranged through IATA-CUBATUR, in the Habana Libre Hotel, or at the consulate of the country to which you are traveling. Below is a partial list of countries with diplomatic representation in Cuba.

Argentina: Calle 36 No. 511 e/5ta. y 7ma. Ave., Miramar. Tel.: 22-5540, 22-5549, 22-5565 and 29-4992.
Austria: Calle 4 No. 511 (esq. a 1ra. Ave.), Miramar. Tel.: 22-5825 and 22-4394.
Belgium: 5ta. Ave. No. 7408 esq. a Calle 76, Miramar. Tel.: 29-6440 and 29-6461.
Brazil: Habana Libre Hotel, L y 23, Vedado. Tel.: 30-5011 ext. 1908 or 1910 and 32-9745 and 32-7013.

Canada: Calle 30 No. 518, esq. a 7ma. Ave., Miramar. Tel.: 2-6421 to 23, 29-3393 and 29-3892.

Czechoslovakia: Ave. Kohly No. 259 e/ 41 y 43, Nuevo Vedado. Tel.: 30-0002, 30-0024 and 30-0046.

Denmark: Paseo de Martí No. 20 apto. 4-C. Tel.: 61-1496 and 61-6610.

Finland: 5ta. Ave. No. 9202, Miramar. Tel.: 2-3795, 2-4098 and 2-6637.

France: Calle 14 No. 312 e/ 3ra. y 5ta., Miramar. Tel.: 29-6048, 29-6143 and 32-8021.

German Democratic Republic: Calle 13 No. 652 e/ A y B, Vedado. Tel.: 3-6626/27 and 3-3584.

Germany, Federal Republic of: Calle 28 No. 313 e/ 3a. y 5ta. Ave., Miramar. Tel.: 22-2560 and 22-2569.

Great Britain: Edificio Bolívar, Cárcel Nos. 101 y 103, Central Havana. Tel.: 61-5681 to 84 and 61-7527.

Guyana: Calle 18 No. 506 e/ 5ta. y 7ma. Ave., Miramar. Tel.: 22-1249 and 22-2494.

India: Calle 21 No. 202 esq. a K, Vedado. Tel.: 32-5169 and 32-5777.

Italy: Paseo No. 606 e/ 25 y 27, Vedado. Tel.: 30-0334, 56, 78 and 90.

Japan: Calle N No. 62 esq. a 15, Vedado. Tel.: 32-3507, 32-5545, 54, 55 and 98.

Mexico: Calle 12 No. 518 e/5ta. y 7ta. Ave., Miramar. Tel.: 2-8198, 2-8634 and 22-1142.

Netherlands: Calle 8 No. 307 e/ 3a. y 5ta. Ave., Miramar. Tel.: 2-6511 and 12, 22-2534.

Nicaragua: 7ma. Ave. No. 1402 esq. a 14, Miramar. Tel.: 2-6810 and 2-6882.

Panama: Calle 26 No. 109 e/ 1ra. y 3ra. Ave., Miramar. Tel.: 22-4096.

Peru: Calle 36 No. 109 e/1ra. y 3ra. Ave., Miramar. Tel.: 29-4477.

Portugal: 5ta. Ave. No. 6604 e/66 y 68, Miramar. Tel.: 2-6871 and 22-2593.

Soviet Union: Calle 13 No. 651 e/ A y B, Vedado. Tel.: 3-3667 and 3-6441.

Spain: Cárcel No. 51 esq. a Zulueta, Central Havana. Tel. 6-4741, 42 and 6-9687.

Sweden: 31 Ave. No. 1411 e/ Calles 14 y 18, Miramar. Tel.: 2-7563, 22-1831 and 29-2871.

Switzerland: 5ta. Ave. No. 2005 e/ Calles 20 y 22, Miramar. Tel.: 2-6452 to 54.

United States Interest Section: Calzada e/ L y M, Vedado. Tel.: 32-0543 to 46, 32-0551 to 59 and 32-9700.

Cuban Tourism Promotion Offices

Argentina
Oficina de Promoción e Información Turística de Cuba
Paraguay 63 2do. piso A
Buenos Aires, Capital Federal
Tel.: 313-4198 and 311-5820
Telex: 18651 FACIB AR

Canada
Bureau de Tourisme de Cuba
440 Dorchester Ouest Bld.
Suite 1402
Montreal, Quebec H2Z 1V1
Tel.: (514) 875-8004/05
Telex: 055-62399 Cubatour-mtl

Cuba Tourist Board
55 Queen Street East. Suite 705
Toronto, Ontario M5H 1R5
Tel.: (416) 362-0700/01/02
Telex: 062-3258 Cubatour-Tor

France
Office de Promotion et Information Touristique de Cuba
24 Rue du Quatre Septembre
Paris 75002
Tel.: (4) 742-5415
Telex: 213709 f cubana

Federal Republic of Germany
Kubanisches Fremdenverkehrsbüro
Steinweg 2
D-6000 Frankfurt-am-Main 1
Tel.: (069) 228-322/23
Telex: 4185577 cutu d

German Democratic Republic
Leninallee 175, 17/06
Lichtemberg 1156, Berlin
Tel.: 372-0461
Telex: 112603 embe d

Italy
Ufficio di Promozione ed Informazione Turistica di Cuba
Via General Fara 30
Terzo Piano
20124 Milan
Tel.: 670-5169
Telex: 320658 cbex i

Mexico
Oficina de Promoción e Información Turística de Cuba
Insurgentes Sur No. 421 esq. Aguascalientes
Complejo Aristos, Edif. B, Local 310
México DF 060100
Tel.: 574-9454 and 574-9651
Telex: 1772900 cubame

USSR
Belgrade Hotel
Smolenskaya 5
Moscow
Tel.: 248-3262
Telex: 414314 cmex su

In Cuba
For specific information and accommodations in Havana,
Varadero and western Cuba, contact:

CUBATUR
Calle 23 No. 156 e/ N y O
Havana 4, Cuba
Tel.: 32-4521
Telex: 511366 and 511243 TUR CU

Individual Tourism Office
Habana Libre Hotel
L y 23, Vedado
Havana 4, Cuba
Tel.: 32-6245, 32-6634 and 32-8512
Telex: 511285 and 511982 TUR CU

For information and accommodations related to conventions, health tourism and eastern Cuba, contact:

CUBANACAN S.A.
Calle 146 e/ 11 y 13, Playa, Rpto. Siboney
Apartado 16046
Havana, Cuba
Telex: 511315 nacan cu

TRAVELING IN CUBA

Flora and Fauna

The largest island in the Greater Antilles, Cuba resembles a somnolent crocodile sunning itself in the Caribbean over a distance of 1250 km. (775 mi.), its body tapering from 190 km. (118 mi.) wide at the eastern head to 30 km. (19 mi.) at the western tail. Including the Isle of Youth (former Isle of Pines) and some 1600 surrounding islets and cays, Cuba is an archipelago with an overall area of 110,922 sq. km. (42,827 sq. mi.) lying 148 km. (90 mi.) south of Key West, Florida; 210 km. (130 mi.) east of the Yucatan Peninsula in Mexico; 140 km. (87 mi.) north of Jamaica; and 77 km. (48 mi.) west of Haiti.

More than 100 beaches dot Cuba's 7500-km. (nearly 5000 mi.) coastline and its offshore waters hold treasures for both fishermen and scuba divers. Three mountain ranges — the Sierra Maestra in the east, with Turquino Peak (highest in the country) rising 1794 m. (5928 ft.) above sea level; the Escambray in the central part of the island; and the Sierra de los Organos in the west, where unique knolls called *mogotes* jut precipitously up from the floor of Viñales Valley — are separated by rolling plains and fertile farmlands that feed people and industry.

Of Cuba's more than 8000 botanical species, its national flower — the fragrant *mariposa* or butterfly jasmine — and the elegant royal palm are most closely associated with the island's history and economy: the *mariposa* was the symbol of patriotism and purity in Cuba's independence wars, when Cuban women wore it in support of the fighters; the royal palm, meanwhile, sheltered the troops and kept them alive as they used its fronds for thatching, its bark for sid-

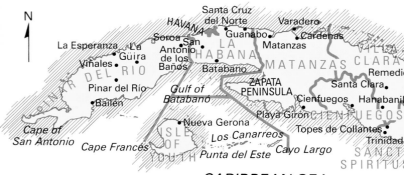

CARIBBEAN SEA

ing and its fruit for food. Cuba is also cactus land and you can view hundreds of varieties growing in the desert-like soil of eastern Baconao Park, in Havana's vast new botanical garden or in the older one outside Cienfuegos founded by Harvard University in 1912.

The island's 300-odd native birds include the red-, white- and blue-feathered Cuban Trogon, the national bird;

and the 62.5-mm.-long (2.5-in.) bee hummingbird, smallest in the world — known locally as *pájaro mosca* (fly), or *zunzuncito* for the swishing sound of its wings. Bird watchers wax ecstatic over the varieties they spot in Cuba's national parks while hunters marvel at the pheasants, guinea hens, mourning doves, common snipes and ducks of all kinds they bag on the island's reserves. Cuba has more than a thousand insect species and the animals (all harmless to man) include several indigenous and nearly extinct mammals — such as the hutía, an edible rodent, and the manatee or sea cow.

By Road

Running down the center of the island, Ocho Vías, the Cuban Thruway, now extends westward from Havana almost to the city of Pinar del Río and eastward to Camagüey over some 700 km. (435 mi.) out of a projected 1000 km. (620 mi.): an eight-lane speedway that considerably reduces driving time and, inevitably, eliminates the charm of coming upon quaint towns and interesting cities.

Paralleling the Thruway is the old two-lane Central Highway: in excellent repair, it is nevertheless the main drag of every town and city it connects and the route for local tractors, buses, old cars, horse-drawn carts and bicycles as well as through traffic.

Hugging the north coast between Havana and Varadero, the Vía Blanca is a fine and wonderfully scenic road. Well-graded blacktop secondary roads, most of them built since 1959, parallel and cross these east-west highways throughout the island. Service stations are prominently located in all towns and cities but are few and far between on the Thruway.

Buses are the chief means of transportation, for both local and long-distance trips. The local bus or *guagua* (pronounced *wa-wa*) costs two five-centavo coins, called *medios*, and you must have the exact fare. Main bus routes in Havana are listed in *GETTING TO KNOW CUBA BY SEEING IT*. Tickets for inter-provincial travel on any carrier must be purchased in advance. Bus tickets are sold one-way rather than round-trip.

TRANSTUR, the national tourist transportation enterprise, has its own fleet of vehicles: five-star Scania buses with 48 seats, bar and toilet, for transporting tourist groups all over the island; and minibuses, station wagons and chauffeur-driven cars for smaller groups and individual tourists. On group tours and optional excursions, an English-speaking guide generally accompanies the English-speaking visitors and transportation is included in the package. Individual tourists can solve transportation needs by attaching themselves to a group for optional excursions, making their own reservations for public transportation, renting a car or taking a taxi.

Rent-a-cars (without chauffeurs) are available in Havana and Varadero on presentation of your own valid driver's license. A Fiat, Lada or VW will cost about $200 USD a week (or $30 a day) including enough gasoline for 100 kilometers (62 miles). These car rentals can be arranged at Havana's International Airport on arrival, at Havanautos' main office in the Capri Hotel (tel. 32-6484), or through Transtur (tel.: 41-8571/72). Any hotel tourism bureau in Havana or Varadero will coordinate your rent-a-car.

Turistaxis leave from and return to major hotels and you pay the driver in foreign currency. Call 79-1940, 79-5665, 79-8613 or 79-8828 for a cab to pick you up anywhere in Havana. You can also flag down a local cab and pay in Cuban pesos (the fare from the Rampa — near most Havana hotels — to Old Havana is about $1.30 plus 40 centavos tip); but taxis drivers assigned to a certain route cannot take passengers elsewhere and the free-wheeling taxis are elusive, to say the least. The older taxis you see on Havana streets operate as one-peso jitneys.

Maps and Addresses

In addition to the maps included in this guide, tourist maps sold in hotel shops will give you a general picture of the island and some of its cities, and a complete, detailed road map of the island is in preparation. Highways and streets are generally well marked — distances are indicated in kilometers: l km. = .62 mi. — and Cubans are helpful with directions, sometimes even when they aren't quite sure.

A Havana address that reads Calle 4 No. 306 e/ 15 y 17, Vedado, means the building is numbered 306 and is on 4th between 15th and 17th Streets in Havana's Vedado district — where most of the hotels, restaurants, theaters, movie houses, cabarets and offices are located. Addresses in the Vedado and Miramar neighborhoods of Havana are especially easy to find because the streets are laid out at right angles with odd numbers crossing even numbers and letters. Street signs are carved in the triangular face of a stone block on sidewalk corners, tacked on the sides of buildings or mounted on posts, depending on the city and the area.

Planes, Boats and Trains

Cubana de Aviación has regular domestic flights to Camagüey, Cayo Largo, Cienfuegos, Havana, Holguín, the Isle of Youth, Manzanillo, Santiago de Cuba and Vara-

dero — all of which have international airports — and to
other cities on the island.

Aero Caribbean Airlines, a charter company with offices
at 23rd and O Streets in Havana, programs its flights to suit
passengers' needs on routes not normally covered, such as
Varadero-Santiago de Cuba, Santiago-Isle of Youth and
others that are even more exotic.

In addition to planes, hydrofoils and ferries connect the
Isle of Youth with the main island, docking at the little
town of Batabanó, on the south shore of Havana Province,
where they are met by buses that bring passengers to and
from the capital.

Cuba's central railroad line has recently been repaired,
new passenger cars have been purchased and, on the 150th
anniversary of the Cuban railroad in 1987, railroad buffs
were offered the option of train travel to selected points of
interest; but, to quote from the daily *Granma*, "the Cuban
railroad is a big elephant that fell down . . . and is finally
trying, with certain difficulties, to get up."

Communications

To make a local call from a public phone, which costs five
centavos or a *medio*, you will probably need several of those
coins. Getting the first one into the box after you hear the
dial tone is easy enough, but the "time up" signal is a brief
blip that requires coin dexterity in order not to be cut off.
You should write down the telephone numbers people give
you since the currently available Havana directory, published in 1979, is woefully out of date (a new one is in preparation) and Information (dial 113) may not have the information you want.

The hotel operator will get a local number for you or
place your long-distance call. If the call is to another country, tell the operator in advance when you want it to go
through, then remind her at the appointed time. See IN
THE HOTEL in the glossary.

Don't try to use the telephone to make reservations.
Have the hotel tourism bureau call for a restaurant or

cabaret table and go personally to the appropriate office to purchase or confirm bus, plane and train reservations. You can send a telegram in English by printing your message on forms provided at the post office (there's a branch in the lobby of the Habana Libre Hotel), where you can also purchase stamps.

Accommodations

A three- to five-star rating for a hotel, motel or villa means you can expect such amenities as hot and cold running water, private baths, restaurant-bar service and air-conditioning. In terms of comfort, the existing pre-revolutionary hotels that offered luxury accommodations in their day have larger rooms and more extensive services than the new prefab structures — and generally cost more, too. Most group travel is geared to a low-cost package with lodgings in three-star hotels pre-booked by tour operators to include some meals and activities.

The hotels outside the tourist network are managed by People's Power, the local administrative government. Most are older, smaller and cheaper than the regular tourist hotels and have the added advantage of being centrally located, but they often lack running water and other conveniences. Many are scheduled for restoration and a few have already been renovated with a fortuitous combination of taste and basic comforts. Cuba has over a hundred campsites, most of them in spectacularly beautiful locations. The facilities are rustic and the price is minimal. Reservations with round-trip transportation can be made at the provincial offices of *Campismo Popular*, paying in Cuban pesos, or at the main office of the appropriate provincial tourism enterprise.

If you're going off on your own after you arrive in Cuba, be sure to make advance hotel reservations through CUBATUR, your base hotel tourism bureau or the individual tourism office in the Habana Libre Hotel. See hotels by city in *GETTING TO KNOW CUBA BY SEEING IT*.

Meals

Cuba's main resort hotels serve buffet breakfasts and dinners that offer a wide variety of fruits and juices, fresh salads and sweet pastries plus a hot main dish. Most also offer à la carte service, as do other hotels. Some campsites have cafetèrias and all have collective kitchens and grocery stores.

Vacationers at Varadero Beach can drop in at any of the seaside villas for a lunch of fresh grilled fish without bothering to change into street clothes. For evening dining out, the resort has any number of places to tempt a gourmet palate. In Havana and other cities, the restaurant ambience is more formal in terms of both service and dress. When you make restaurant reservations through the hotel tourism bureau, you will pay a minimum which is deducted from the final bill on presentation of your reservation slip. There is no service charge in Cuban restaurants and tips are expected. Except in Varadero, where everything is geared to tourism, you may want to have a few pesos on hand for the ice cream parlor and sno-cone cart that accept Cuban money only.

Restaurant service is generally slow — except for the buffets, of course — but the food is generally fresh and well prepared. Restaurants worth trying are listed by city and *Miniconversation No. 10* tells you how to order from a restaurant menu.

In Case of Illness

Cuba has the most advanced and widely distributed health care in Latin America. Moreover, it's all free for residents and partly free for visitors. Resorts and the bigger city hotels have first aid stations for immediate free attention to minor illnesses or injuries. If further treatment is required, the patient will be taken to the local polyclinic or hospital (first visit free of charge). Over-the-counter and prescription medicine can be purchased at any pharmacy. See *Miniconversation No. 8*.

GETTING TO KNOW CUBA THROUGH ITS HISTORY

CONQUISTADORES, INDIANS AND SLAVES

When Columbus reached the northeastern shore of Cuba — which he described as "the most beautiful land ever seen" — on October 27, 1492, he was certain that "where there is such marvelous scenery, there must be much from which profit can be made." But instead of great cities and fabulous wealth, his scouts encountered a settlement of Taíno Indians, who lived in rude huts they called *bohíos*, furnished only with *hamacas* for sleeping. The Taínos and sub-Taínos first reached Cuba from what is now the Dominican Republic around 1100, the last Indian group to migrate to the island from South America. They were ceramicists and weavers as well as fishermen and farmers, more advanced than either the Ciboney fishermen- farmers who lived on the southern coast or the primitive Guanahatabey hunters and cave dwellers of the northwest, who inhabited the island as early as 3500 B.C. The peaceful, friendly Taínos feasted the Spaniards with the fish and small animals they caught and the few plants they grew, including a leaf they dried, rolled and smoked: the Europeans were thus introduced to tobacco.

The Spanish Crown, however, wanted gold (tobacco would come later); so in 1512, Diego Velázquez, who had become the richest Spanish planter on nearby Hispaniola, was commissioned to conquer Cuba for Spain and search for the precious metal.

The Indians at the eastern tip of Cuba were warned of the impending invasion. An Indian chief named Hatuey, who had escaped after fighting the Spaniards on Hispaniola, told them: "These Europeans worship a very

17

covetous sort of God. They will exact immense treasures of us and will use their utmost endeavors to reduce us to a miserable state of slavery or else put us to death."

When Velázquez and some 300 other Spanish adventurers, including Hernando Cortés, came ashore and planted a Cross in the name of the Crown, they were greeted by a rain of arrows from Hatuey's men, who used tactics that have since come to be known as guerrilla warfare to pin the Spaniards down for nearly three months in the place they named Baracoa. Hatuey was finally captured and burned at the stake, his followers rounded up and killed.

Velázquez and his men proceeded westward, slaughtering peaceful Indians as they went or forcing them to mine what gold was found. Bartolomé de las Casas, the priest who accompanied the conquistadores, soon became known as the Apostle of the Indians because he spoke out against the horrors he witnessed.

Whole tribes committed suicide. Others managed to escape to the mountains and raid the colonizers from there. Among these so-called *cimarrones* — a name later applied to runaway slaves — were the Cuban Indian chief Guamá, his wife Habaguanex and his sixty brothers, who fought Spanish troops in the mountains of eastern Cuba for 11 years (1522-1533) in the last major Indian uprising. In just two decades, an indigenous population of more than 100,000 had been virtually exterminated. Meanwhile, the conquistadores had established seven important villas as they moved from east to west: Baracoa, Santiago de Cuba, Bayamo, Puerto Príncipe (now Camagüey), Sancti Spíritus, Trinidad and San Cristóbal de la Habana.

The first large-scale slave shipment reached Cuba in 1524, when 300 Africans were brought in to work the Jagua gold mine. Eight years later, the first recorded slave revolt took place at the Jobabo mine near Bayamo; and, five years after that, when French pirates attacked Havana, the slaves there rose up and sacked the city. Countless other revolts took place before slavery was finally abolished in 1880.

PIRATES, SMUGGLERS AND *VEGUEROS*

Because of its fine harbor, Havana quickly became Spain's navigation center in the Americas. A floating population from other Spanish colonies waited in Havana for the return trip to Seville — the only trade route permitted by the Crown — and taverns and inns sprang up to cater to troops, crews and adventurers. Tobacco was sold in the city and shipped to Seville along with gold and silver from Mexico and Peru. Spanish ships were built and repaired with the island's fine wood and their crews took aboard dried meat, cassava bread and yucca in Havana as fare for the voyage.

By the 17th century, the island's population was composed of an incipient urban and landed bourgeoisie, peasants who had immigrated chiefly from Andalucía, Galicia and the Canary Islands, the few remaining Indians and the first waves of Africans. In Havana, blacks were specifically barred from owning taverns but made a business of entertaining transient sailors in their rustic huts, providing food, drink, games, and music. Thus the African drum accompanied the Spanish guitar almost from the start.

Throughout the 16th and 17th centuries, the Caribbean was the frontier that European powers battled to control as an extension of continental conflicts. Although fortresses were built to defend Havana, Santiago de Cuba and smaller Cuban ports as well, piracy and buccaneering were constant threats until they were ended by the Peace of Rijswijk in 1697, eliminating one factor that had slowed Cuba's development.

The other, and far more important, factor was the iron grip the Spanish Crown and clergy maintained on the economy through production and trade restrictions, duties, taxes and tithes. A total monopoly on tobacco led to big-time smuggling, especially in the eastern town of Bayamo, where local planters and clergy traded the prized leaf, as well as hides and meat, for textiles and manufactured goods brought by French, English and Dutch ships officially banned from Cuban ports.

The tobacco growers, or *vegueros*, around Havana had greater difficulty selling their product to smugglers and their only alternative to total ruin was to fight the Spanish monopoly. In 1717, they organized the first armed insurrection against Spanish restrictions. They revolted again three years later and again in 1723, when 500 *vegueros* destroyed the tobacco fields of growers who had sold to the monopoly. Nine of the rebels were killed when Spanish troops fired on them and another 12 were captured and immediately executed by order of the Governor. The monopoly, of course, continued.

AFTER THE BRITISH, THINGS WERE NEVER THE SAME

In 1762, the British seized Havana and occupied it for nearly a year, during which time they opened the port to unrestricted trade. They sold merchandise and slaves and engaged in commerce with their American colonies to the north, laying the bases for increased sugar production (until then, only Havana and Matanzas had shipped small amounts to Spain) that required still more slaves.

After Havana was returned to Spain in exchange for the Florida Peninsula, it became clear that the old trade restrictions could not be reimposed. When the North American colonies declared their independence from Britain in 1776, Spain supported them and permitted North American ships to trade with Cuba. The idea of colonies becoming independent countries was not lost on the Cubans. Many criollos (Cuban-born descendants of Spaniards) already had serious differences with Spain's administrative, military and clerical representatives, who made fortunes in Cuba at their expense. In 1789, the French Revolution erupted and its egalitarian ideas spread throughout Latin America. Thomas Paine's persuasive defense of the French Revolution in *Rights of Man*, which also carried the text of

the American Declaration of Independence, was translated
into Spanish and circulated secretly in Cuba. Then, in 1791,
the Haitian Revolution exploded and the first republic in
the Americas governed by former slaves was established.

SUGAR, SLAVES AND REBELLION

Some of the ruined Haitian sugarcane and coffee planters
fled to Cuba with their slaves, adding to Cuba's ethnic and
cultural mix. And Cuba soon took over from Haiti as the
main producer of sugar and importer of slaves. Some
33,400 slaves entered Cuba before 1791, when the island
exported a mere 17,000 tons of sugar. Between 1791 and
1805, more than 91,000 slaves entered Cuba through
Havana alone; and, from 1821 to 1831 — sugar boom years
— 600,000 slaves were brought into Cuba and the black
population outnumbered the white.

They belonged to the Bantu, Congolese, Dahoman,
Mandingo and, especially, Yoruba groupings of West Africa whose myths were based on the worship of powerful
gods and goddesses. The Catholic Church in Cuba, while a
bulwark of slavocracy, saved both white and black souls
and the slaves were able to recognize in this new religion
paler counterparts of their own gods and goddesses —
whom they worshipped by their African names. *Santería*,
as this synthesis came to be called, was viewed by the slave
owners and their Church with a certain tolerance.

Life was harsh on the big western plantations where
slaves cut sugarcane with machetes from sunrise to sunset
and were locked into crowded barracks at night. Any sign
of rebellion was brutally punished. Runaways were frequent, and these *cimarrones* banded together in fortified
communities called *palenques*, deep in the mountains.

Cuban slaves nevertheless had certain advantages over
those in other countries, such as the United States. They
could marry and have families and they could also own and
sell crops, crafts and property, using the accumulated capital to purchase their own freedom and that of their im-

mediate family. Children born of the union of a slave and a colonist were automatically free. Cuba's many free blacks kept their beliefs and customs alive in their own organizations, called *cabildos*. At the same time they held both menial and professional jobs, contributing their skills and talents to building the country and developing its culture. These free blacks were also in a better position than the slaves to organize insurrections.

In 1812, a young free black carpenter in Havana named José Antonio Aponte — who was aware of revolutionary ideas and had made contact with some sympathetic Haitians — organized a national conspiracy to abolish slavery. The conspiracy was discovered and Aponte was hanged with eight of his co-conspirators. Aponte's head was exhibited in an iron cage in front of his house and his hand was nailed to a street wall. During 1843 and 1844, a series of slave rebellions took place on the big Matanzas sugarcane plantations. Then the rumor spread that free blacks, slaves and some whites were conspiring to rise up and establish a republic based on equality for all. On the basis of this rumor, Spanish authorities unleashed the most brutal repression in the island's history: *La Escalera*.

More than 4000 people — mainly blacks — were arrested, tied to ladders (*escaleras*) and lashed until they confessed or died. Seventy-eight people were executed and nearly 1700 imprisoned or exiled. Hundreds died under the lash. Among the free blacks executed was the talented poet-artisan Gabriel de la Concepción Valdés, known as Plácido, whose only crime was that his poetry affirmed a hatred of tyranny.

The abolitionist movement in Cuba was literally decapitated as a result of *La Escalera*, but fear of future conspiracies led to clamor for an end to the slave trade and it was halted the following year.

Then, in a last desperate effort to save a decadent slave system, many landowners in Cuba began to import indentured servants from China through agencies set up in Portuguese Macao and British Hong Kong. Between 1853 and

1873, more than 132,000 Chinese "coolies" were shipped to Cuba under eight-year contracts to do whatever agricultural, commercial or domestic work their masters assigned them at a wage of four pesos a month. Thirteen percent of them died on the way or soon after arrival, but many managed to finish their contracts and establish small businesses, especially in Havana.

CUBA'S TEN YEARS' WAR
OF INDEPENDENCE (1868-1878)

As Simón Bolívar freed most of South America, Spain made alternate demands and concessions to hold Cuba. It was able to do so because of the fanatical support of the petit-bourgeois *peninsulares* organized as Volunteers, mainly in Havana, and because the opposition was divided. The reformists wanted Cuba to remain a Spanish colony with home rule. The annexationists, mainly the big sugar planters in the west, believed they could best protect the slave economy they needed by becoming part of the United States. The independence protagonists, headed by the smaller landowners in the east, wanted to sever Cuba's colonial ties. What brought these currents into turbulent warfare was the crisis that began in 1857 — Cuba was then exporting 612,000 tons of sugar a year — when the bottom fell out of the sugar market. This meant ruin for the small plantations with few slaves and generally outmoded equipment, mainly in the east.

On October 10, 1868, Carlos Manuel de Céspedes freed the slaves on his sugar plantation La Demajagua, near Manzanillo in what is now Granma Province, and led them into the first battle of the Cuban War of Independence at Yara. Cattle raiser, sugarcane plantation owner, slaveholder, lawyer, poet and traveler, Céspedes had been conspiring with other eastern landowners who also joined the struggle, each with his former slaves and neighboring farmers and tradesmen. From the start, then, the independence fighters were organized into semi-autonomous divisions structured from top to bottom, composed of rural and urban whites, mulattos, free blacks and slaves led by the landed gentry.

The Spaniards referred to the insurrectionists as *mambís*, a word they had learned from their African slaves. In Congolese it means dirty, vile, abominable and bad. But the Afro-Cuban rebels turned the slur into a badge of honor as they wielded their machetes in hand-to-hand cavalry combats with Spanish troops.

The Mambís quickly took the city of Bayamo, riding in to the stirring strains of what is now Cuba's national anthem, written by Pedro Figueredo, Bayamese musician, writer, lawyer and revolutionary. Parading in dress uniform: long-sleeved, tucked white *guayabera* (typical Cuban country shirt of that period and an all-round favorite today), with a red scarf at the neck, the rebels were cheered by the enthusiastic townspeople. And when the Spanish sent a large force to reconquer the city, the residents burned it to the ground rather than permit it to fall into Spanish hands again.

In Havana, the reaction to the declaration of war and, especially, to the burning of Bayamo was violent: Volunteers destroyed the homes, businesses and cafés owned by Cubans suspected of sympathizing with the revolution. So great was the terror that everyone who could afford to do so left for the United States. Between February and September of 1869, more than 100,000 Cubans fled the island. The property and other possessions they left behind — valued at some $125 million in all — were confiscated and handed over to the Volunteers.

Among those arrested in 1869 was a 16-year-old student named José Martí, who had expressed his support of independence in a note written to a classmate. Although it was his first open act of defiance, Martí was already committed to the ideals of freedom and independence he had discussed with his teacher and friend Rafael María Mendive. Indeed, it was Mendive who had made it possible for Martí to continue in school when his parents were unable to pay the cost. Martí's father was a poor ex-sergeant whose wife also came from a humble Spanish family and they had seven younger girls to feed and clothe as well as José.

For his crime, Martí was sentenced to six years of forced labor in the government stone quarries, where the prisoners wore chains around their ankles as they hacked at the rock under a broiling tropical sun. After six months of this brutal work that left him scarred for life, Martí — through the efforts of his father's army friends — was transferred to prison on the Isle of Pines. He was deported to Spain in 1871, the year the Volunteers in Havana forced the execution on November 27 of eight medical students falsely accused of profaning a tomb. Martí never forgot either the harsh prison conditions or the fate of those students and both served to strengthen his commitment to freedom and justice.

In Spain, Martí continued his studies, earning university degrees in law and philosophy. He also launched his writing career with an article on the treatment of political prisoners in Cuba, began to expound his ideas in public speeches and organized demonstrations such as the rally commemorating the Cuban medical students. He was unable to return to Cuba but longed to be closer to events there, so he went to Mexico where he continued to write plays and poetry and began working as a journalist. He visited Cuba briefly under an assumed name, then returned to Mexico and Guatemala. By this time, Martí was a well-known figure in Latin-American literary and political circles and among exiled Cubans. One of them, Carmen Zayas Bazán, became his wife.

After ten years of fighting, the social class that had started the war was liquidated and serious differences had arisen among the leadership. The giant mills in the west that produced 80 percent of Cuban sugar remained untouched by the war; but in eastern Cuba where the fighting took place, more than 100 sugarmills as well as crops and homes were destroyed and many people were destitute. When Spain proposed a general amnesty in return for the surrender of the rebel troops, the majority accepted the agreement, known as the Zanjón Pact.

Only General Antonio Maceo y Grajales, the Bronze Titan of the east, believed the rebels could continue fighting a war of attrition and win it, as he stated in his stirring Protest of Baraguá.

Maceo and his ten brothers were born of free black parents in Santiago de Cuba. Through Maceo's early interest in politics the whole family joined the liberation struggle. Maceo rose rapidly in the ranks of the Mambí Army and was the chief practitioner of guerrilla tactics that served him in hundreds of battles. Self-educated, Maceo read voraciously and promoted reading and discussion in his camps, which were organized with hospitals, workshops, stores and living quarters for the men and their families. His wife María Cabrales and his mother Mariana Grajales, who said she would gladly give all her sons for Cuba's independence — and did — both worked as nurses in his camps.

Maceo and his troops were unable to hold out alone with the Protest of Baraguá, so the Ten Years' War ended and Maceo left for exile in Jamaica.

Under the general amnesty, Martí returned to Cuba along with many other independence supporters, among them General Calixto García, who led the Little War that flared up briefly and died out in 1880. Martí's support for it forced him into exile again, this time to the United States.

THE NECESSARY WAR (1895)

Between 1880, when slavery was abolished in Cuba, and 1895, when the Second War of Independence was launched, US investments in Cuba were heavy. Although 93.5 percent of the sugarmills were directly owned by Cubans and Spaniards, the United States controlled all the trade and, by 1890 — due to the competition of European beet sugar — was the only customer for Cuban cane sugar. With US investments, technological advancements were introduced in Cuban mills and housing and public works were constructed in urban areas. But the agricultural system remained as backward as ever and the canefield workers — former slaves and contracted laborers — were still the exploited pawns in a one-crop economy. Meanwhile, Spanish colonial repression and corruption continued to choke the Cuban economy and throttle the Cuban people.

Martí realized that this situation could change only if Cuba won its freedom. As time went on, he became more and more convinced that independence had to be attained "in time," as he wrote in his last letter, "to keep the United States from expanding through the Antilles and falling with even greater force on our lands of America."

His humble background, his broad education and his experience as an exile made him keenly aware of the social problems of the Cuban emigrés among whom he lived in the United States and certain that their solution depended on solving the national question. With his multifaceted talents, he wrote articles, essays, pamphlets, children's stories and plays, but his life was devoted, in the deepest sense, to organizing his people for what he believed was the necessary war for independence.

In 1892, Martí founded the Cuban Revolutionary Party, loosely structured in local clubs of Cuban exiles in New York and among the highly organized cigar makers in Florida. The Party's goal was national revolution to establish an independent republic. Acceptance of that goal was the sole criterion for membership, since it was Martí's aim to unite all Cubans, regardless class or race. He was particularly alarmed at the divisiveness of the racist slanders against Maceo, whom he considered "a symbol of national integration."

The Party paper *Patria*, which Martí edited, constantly espoused ideas of equality and unity in an anti-imperialist independence movement controlled by civilians. Martí was also a spell-binding orator who conveyed the passion of a conviction his audience shared. The Party clubs elected him their Delegate or civilian representative and he then polled each club to determine the military leadership of the war. General Maximo Gómez, the legendary Dominican of the Ten Years' War, was appointed Commander in Chief and his friend Antonio Maceo was named Lieutenant General of the Liberation Army. Maintaining the important network of communications between the exiles and the revolutionary forces in Cuba was delegated to the Afro-Cuban journalist Juan Gualberto Gómez. Funds for the war came mainly from Cuban workers in the United States, who contributed 10 percent or more of their wages to pay for arms and ammunition.

Martí was the genius and moving spirit in this great pro-independence organization, but he also believed he should take an active part in the fighting. He and Gómez came ashore at Playitas, on the southern coast of Cuba between Guantánamo and Baracoa. Maceo landed at Duaba, northwest of Baracoa. On May 19, 1895, Martí was killed in a cavalry skirmish near Dos Ríos. A year later, after a brilliant campaign of battles fought from eastern Oriente to western Pinar del Río, Maceo, like all the men in his family, was killed. With him died his aide-de-camp Panchito Gómez, son of the Commander in Chief. In spite of these and other terrible battle losses and the death by starvation of nearly 200,000 civilian victims of Spanish Captain General Valeriano Weyler's population reconcentration policy, the liberators steadily gained ground.

US INTERVENTION (1898) AND MANIPULATION

The United States government, with a close eye on its economic and strategic interests in Cuba, withheld recognition of the independence forces while William Randolph Hearst's "yellow press" whipped up sentiment against Spain. When the US Consul in Havana asked his government to send a warship to protect US lives and property, the battleship *Maine* was promptly dispatched, arriving in Havana harbor on January 24, 1898. In the early morning hours of February 15, it was mysteriously blown up and

266 of its crew members — nearly all blacks — were killed. The perpetrators of the crime were never discovered, though the prevailing theory is that the US itself was responsible. At the time, however, the US press openly blamed Spain, creating a climate of hysteria in which Congress, on April 25, 1898, declared war on that country.

With the help of General Calixto García's independence forces, the US fleet blockaded Santiago de Cuba and the troops landed accompanied by a battery of foreign correspondents who duly described the glamour and glory of war. An exception was writer Stephen Crane who reported first for Pulitzer's *World* and then for Hearst's *Journal*. Landing with the Marines in Guantánamo, Crane spent four days in the thick of the fighting, was officially cited for coolness under fire at Cuzco, witnessed the inland ambush at Las Guásimas and was at San Juan Hill when Teddy Roosevelt's volunteer Rough Riders — idolized in the press — fought alongside Mambí troops. The carnage of battle and the thousands of deaths from malaria, yellow fever and dysentery were what struck Crane, however, and from Havana he cabled: "In our next war, our first bit of strategy should be to have the Army and the Navy combine in an assault on Washington. If we could once take and sack Washington, the rest of the conflict would be simple."

When Spain surrendered to US General Shafter on July 17, 1898, the Cuban troops who had been so instrumental in the victory were barred from entering Santiago de Cuba and the American flag was raised in place of the Spanish. Under the terms of the peace treaty, Spain formally handed the island over to the United States and a US Military Governor replaced the Spanish Captain General. General Máximo Gómez was stripped of his title and the Liberation Army was disarmed and disbanded by the Cuban Legislative Assembly, following orders given by the new military occupiers.

In 1901, when the Cuban Constitutional Assembly met to draw up the basic document for the new republic, its members were presented with a Constitution that had been drafted in Washington, complete with the infamous Platt Amendment. The amendment gave the United States the right to intervene in Cuban affairs any time it so desired, establish permanent naval bases on the island, make treaties and control Cuba's foreign indebtedness; and it left ownership of the Isle of Pines to "future adjustment by treaty." A majority of the delegates balked at approving such conditions, but US General Leonard Wood threatened continued military occupation and they had no choice but to give in. The Isle of Pines finally became a part of Cuban territory in 1934 but the United States still maintains a Naval Base at Guantánamo Bay in eastern Cuba.

When the Republic of Cuba was constituted in 1902, the only concession to the Liberation Army was the adoption of its blue-and-white striped emblem with the red triangle and a single white star as the country's official flag.

Although the Constitution of the Republic recognized Martí's precept of equality for all Cubans, in practice blacks were excluded from elective and appointive government posts and from all kinds of privately-owned businesses.

The Colored Independence Party was established to fight such exclusion but was outlawed in 1910 by an amendment to the Electoral Law declaring political associations formed by people of one class or color to be illegal. After two years of fruitless efforts to overturn that amendment, an "armed protest" was organized against it. The action took place near Guantánamo, where party members peacefully occupied the small town of La Maya without harming anyone. The tactic backfired, however, and powerful forces of retaliation were set in motion, fanned by the flames of racism. US troops from Guantánamo Base occupied towns on the outskirts of Guantánamo and Santiago de Cuba, while Cuban troops pursued the rebels, hunting down and slaughtering 3000 of them in the bloodiest repression of blacks since *La Escalera*.

CRISIS, DICTATORSHIP AND REVOLUTION

Backed by their government and their army, US business-men rushed into Cuba to buy up land, sugarmills, cigar factories and railroads and run the island for their own profit. US investments in Cuba rose from $50 million in 1895 to $200 million in 1910 and $1.5 billion in 1925. Cuban presidents came and went through a revolving door of corruption and fraud while a one-crop economy placed the country and its workers at the mercy of the sugar market.

During and immediately after World War I, when there was no competition from European beet sugar, prices of Cuban cane sugar soared in what was called the "dance of millions." New mansions, hotels, and gambling casinos were built as Havana became the Latin-American center of gambling, prostitution and corruption. In 1924, when the price of sugar had dropped to three cents a pound on the New York market and the island's economy was in crisis, a crooked politician named Gerardo Machado spent a half million dollars to win the Cuban presidential election.

People took to the streets with economic and political demands. The repercussions of the Bolshevik Revolution in Russia were visible in the militancy of the students, whose charismatic leader Julio Antonio Mella was a founder of Cuba's first Marxist Party; in strikes led by the National Workers Federation; and in the seizure of sugarmills and distribution of land to peasants in the countryside.

As the revolutionary tide swelled, Machado usurped constitutional powers and became a bloody dictator, repressing strikes, closing schools, banning public meetings, assassinating opponents and murdering ordinary people. Mella, exiled in Mexico, was killed by Machado's henchmen.

Events came to a head in a gigantic national strike in August 1933 that forced Machado to flee the country. In the succeeding struggle for power, a Provisional Revolutionary Government was formed in which 26-year-old Antonio

Guiteras Holmes — former student leader and fighter against Machado — held key posts and pushed through radical reforms. But the government fell after 100 days, as an Army sergeant named Fulgencio Batista, backed by US Ambassador Sumner Welles, maneuvered to control the situation. Guiteras continued to speak out against imperialism and repression but concluded that armed struggle alone could change the situation. On the night of May 7, 1935, as he was waiting for a boat to take him to Mexico to organize that struggle, Guiteras was killed by Army soldiers.

Pressures from the people continued, leading to such concessions as the 1940 Constitution, a liberal document that was never implemented. For the average Cuban, life remained as hard as ever while government corruption and speculation increased during the years before, during and after World War II.

Finally, in 1952, the Orthodox Party succeeded in organizing masses of people for a real change and seemed destined to win the election. One of the younger members of that party was a recently graduated lawyer and former student leader named Fidel Castro Ruz, 26-year-old son of an Oriente plantation owner.

In order to prevent the election of a progressive government, Batista seized power in a coup on March 10, 1952, and imposed a seven-year dictatorship of unprecedented brutality.

The first major blow against the Batista dictatorship was struck on July 26, 1953. Castro and 125 young followers used the carnival in Santiago de Cuba as a cover to attack the Moncada Garrison, Cuba's second largest. The attack failed and many of the rebels were captured and tortured to death. Fidel and a few others managed to escape into the mountains, but they were all rounded up in the manhunt that followed. The lieutenant who arrested Fidel saved his life by taking him to a civilian rather than a military prison, where Batista had ordered that ten rebels be killed for every soldier who had died.

Public outcry forced a trial of the survivors but all were convicted. Tried separately and in secret, Castro acted as his own lawyer. His eloquent defense was smuggled out of jail and published as *History Will Absolve Me*, the basic program of the revolution. He was sentenced to 15 years and transferred to the Model Prison — a copy of the one in Joliet, Illinois, USA — on the Isle of Pines, where most of the other defendants were also sent. The two women who participated in the attack, Haydée Santamaría and Melba Hernández, were put behind bars in the National Women's Prison in Guanajay, near Havana.

On May 15, 1955, in response to a well-organized amnesty campaign, they were all released. Fidel and many of his comrades were soon forced to leave for Mexico, where they began training for the coming struggle in Cuba. It was there that Ernesto Che Guevara met Fidel, joined the 26th of July Movement and became one of the 82 men who sailed for Cuba on the cabin cruiser *Granma*, which landed at Las Coloradas Beach in Oriente Province on December 2, 1956.

Initial skirmishes reduced the group to the 12 survivors who set up the first guerrilla base in the Sierra Maestra Mountains and established contact with Frank País, head of underground activities for the 26th of July Movement in Santiago de Cuba. Working with Frank was a young rebel named Vilma Espín (now head of the Federation of Cuban Women and wife of Fidel's younger brother Raúl), who later recalled their first meeting with the rebels in the Sierra in February 1957:

"The Rebel Army was still very small, just over 20 with the peasants who had joined the surviving expeditionaries. They were a ragged, unshaven bunch but full of life and toughened by what they had been through. Fidel, optimistic and confident as always, immediately drew up a manifesto for distribution to the people. He asked Frank to send up 50 of Santiago's toughest comrades in the struggle and that first group was ready ten days after we got back. We sent our finest comrades, all well trained and equipped with uniforms, backpacks and boots. And we sent the same equipment for the men already in the Sierra. . . . ''

As the Rebel Army grew, it set up schools, hospitals and workshops and established agrarian reform in the areas it controlled, maintaining absolute respect for the long-exploited *guajiros* — as Cuban peasants are called — and the land they worked, usually as squatters. The rebels addressed each other and their neighbors as *compañero*, meaning comrade and friend, a term you hear everywhere in modern-day Cuba.

Meanwhile, the rebels stepped up their offensive against enemy troops in the Sierra Maestra and, by the end of the year, had the enemy on the defensive. News of their victories was broadcast over Radio Rebelde — for which Che was largely responsible — and heard clandestinely all over the island.

In the cities, actions such as the daring 1957 attack on Havana's Presidential Palace — in a frustrated attempt to kill Batista — and the general strike of 1958 were organized in support of the *barbudos*, as the bearded guerrilla fighters came to be called.

The decisive battle and turning point in the guerrilla war came at El Jigüe, in July of 1958, when a 241-man battalion surrendered to Major Fidel Castro after a 10-day seige. The enemy launched a counteroffensive, which failed, and the rebel forces continued to advance: Fidel's column pressed toward Santiago, Raúl moved into northern Oriente, Che and Camilo Cienfuegos crossed Camagüey into Las Villas Province, where Che's rebel forces stormed Santa Clara, derailing an armored train bringing reinforcements for Batista's troops.

In the early morning hours of January 1, 1959, Batista and his cronies fled the country. Fidel drove from Santiago to Havana, through throngs of cheering people, to accept the surrender of Batista's former stronghold, Camp Columbia. The Cuban revolution had triumphed after 100 years of struggle.

A NEW ERA

When the revolution came to power in 1959, 23 percent of adults were illiterate, 25 percent of the male population was unemployed, and the economy was controlled by the latifundist system of great plantations run by primitive agricultural methods using low-cost labor.

One of the first laws passed by the new government was the Agrarian Reform Law of May 17, 1959, which limited the size of farms by turning the land over to those who worked it and nationalizing the big plantations. This, more than anything else, brought down the wrath of the Cuban and foreign bourgeoisie, who collaborated in calumnious propaganda, acts of sabotage and the training of mercenary troops for an attack against Cuba.

Meanwhile, Cuba was turning fortresses into schools and setting up a free educational program launched with the massive literacy campaign of 1961 that reduced adult illiteracy to 3 percent. The government also established medical posts in rural areas and free health care for all. Rents were drastically reduced and new housing and recreational facilities were built — which also helped provide new jobs. By outlawing racial discrimination, the new government was able to provide equal access to all these benefits. National poet Nicolás Guillén summed it all up in a poem entitled *"Tengo"* (I Have):

> I have, let's see:
> that being Black
> I can be stopped by no one at
> the door of a dancing hall or bar. . . .
>
> I have, let's see:
> that I have learned to read,
> to count,
> I have that I have learned to write,
> and to think
> and to laugh.
> I have that now I have
> a place to work

and earn
what I have to eat.
I have, let's see:
I have what was coming to me.

Blockade and Harassment

On January 3, 1961, the United States broke diplomatic relations with the Cuban government and imposed an
economic blockade of the island which is still in effect.

Then, on April 17, 1961, a mercenary brigade of counterrevolutionary Cubans trained and equipped under US
Presidents Eisenhower and Kennedy and transported to
the coast of Cuba in US warships, landed at the Bay of Pigs
— where it was defeated in 72 hours. On the eve of the battle, Prime Minister Fidel Castro announced that Cuba
would become the first socialist state in the Americas. The
mercenaries taken prisoner at the Bay of Pigs were exchanged for medicine and tractors Cuba was unable to purchase because of the US blockade.

In 1962, Cuba made an agreement with the Soviet Union
for the installation of nuclear missiles to protect the island's
coast from the US warships that constantly hovered on the
horizon. Outraged, the United States threatened to fire its
powerful missiles at Cuba unless the Soviets withdrew
those on the island. With the world on the brink of war, the
Soviets removed the missiles from Cuba and the United
States removed the missiles it had in Turkey. US President
John Kennedy also made a verbal pledge to Soviet leader
Nikita Khrushchev that Cuba's territorial integrity would
be respected. Violations of that commitment have ranged
from US overflights and naval maneuvers to infiltrations by
saboteurs and attempts to assassinate Fidel Castro — all
documented in US Congressional testimony.

Following the missile crisis, the US prodded the Organization of American States to expel Cuba, which it did on
July 26, 1963, the tenth anniversary of the attack on the
Moncada. Since then, the OAS has lost much of its moral
and political prestige, and Cuba now has diplomatic and
trade relations with most of its members.

Blockade and harassment by the United States continue unabated, forcing the Cuban government to assign funds and manpower to defense that could otherwise be used for development. This factor, added to the general world economic crisis, has resulted in hardships and shortages for the Cuban people along with real and palpable advances in education, medicine, science and the arts. The aid and solidarity of the European socialist countries, especially the Soviet Union, have been important factors in Cuba's ability to create a stable sociopolitical climate and establish a base for development in spite of the enmity of its great northern neighbor.

Defense and Organizations

As a deterrent to attack, Cuba has built a formidable defense system based on a well-trained and equipped military force backed by a people's militia of more than a million volunteer combat trainees. Fidel Castro is Commander in Chief of the Armed Forces while his brother Raúl is Chief of Staff and Minister of Defense.

Cubans, almost to the last man, woman and child, are members of and usually active participants in one or more mass organization. The Committees for the Defense of the Revolution (CDR), which operate on a block level, are the neighborhood link in health, education, security and work and the electoral base of People's Power. The trade unions, to which all workers belong, are organized by industry and represented in the umbrella Central Organization of Trade Unions (CTC). The National Association of Small Farm Owners (ANAP) represents farmers' interests. The Federation of Cuban Women (FMC) initiates educational and job training programs for women and pushes for their full and equal participation in all aspects and at all levels of Cuban life, fighting the evils of *machismo* in the work place and in the home. Students have their own mass organizations, from the young Pioneers through the Federation of Senior High School Students (FEEM) and the Federation of University Students (FEU).

Party and Government

The Communist Party of Cuba (PCC) was established in 1965 as the country's highest policy-making body, with Fidel Castro at its head. The Central Committee of the PCC sets economic and political guidelines and makes the final decisions on their implementation. Party members, selected from all walks of life on the basis of their dedication, are expected to be critical and self-critical and set an example as workers and human beings. The Union of Young Communists (UJC) actively supports Party policy and serves as the training ground for Party membership.

The Cuban Constitution (available in English) was approved by plebiscite in 1976. It sets forth the basic principles of Cuban society and the rights, privileges and responsibilities of citizens and their government.

Administratively, Cuba is divided into 14 provinces: from west to east, Pinar del Río, City of Havana, Havana, Matanzas, Villa Clara, Cienfuegos, Sancti Spíritus, Ciego de Avila, Camagüey, Las Tunas, Holguín, Granma, Santiago de Cuba and Guantánamo; and the special municipality of the Isle of Youth, off the southern coast of Havana Province.

Administrative authority is vested in the municipal, provincial and national bodies of People's Power, whose local delegates are elected by and responsible to their neighborhood constituencies. From them come the Municipal, Provincial and National Assembly delegates. The National Assembly of People's Power elects the Council of State, supreme governing body, which in turn selects its Council of Ministers. Fidel Castro is President of both Councils and Raúl Castro is his second.

The Economy

Economically, sugar is still king, though it is now a highly technical and largely mechanized agroindustry. The *zafra*, as the sugarcane harvest is called, runs roughly from November through May and yields an annual eight to nine million tons of sugar to meet both domestic and trade commitments. Although 65 percent of cane cutting is now mechanized, it is still symbolized by the individual *machetero* wielding his sharp machete through the field. Fewer than 80,000 *macheteros* now work in the harvest — compared to 350,000 in 1970 — and the best of them cut as many as five million arrobas (1 arroba equals 25 pounds) a season.

Most of the big modern sugarmills are fueled by sugarcane bagasse, permitting Cuba to export some of the oil it imports from the Soviet Union. Small amounts of offshore oil have been discovered and a more promising vein was recently tapped under Cárdenas Bay, near Varadero Beach. Meanwhile, Cuba's first atomic energy plant is under construction, with Soviet aid, in the seaside city of Cienfuegos.

Agriculture has been diversified to feed a growing population and complemented with new industries that meet the country's domestic and export needs. Economic planning is centralized but administration and operation are local.

Sugar is the main export product but minerals — especially nickel, of which Cuba has the world's largest reserves — seafood, citrus fruits, coffee and tobacco are also important. Since Cuba needs to increase exports to earn hard currency for continuing development, the emphasis in all branches of the economy is on quality products for export while replacing imports with domestic production. Important resources have been designated for remodeling tourist installations and improving services in this sector which is now the country's third source of foreign income and is expected to be in first place by the end of the century.

Eighty percent of Cuba's trade is with other socialist countries, the remainder with Canada, Western Europe, Japan and Latin America.

The Fabric of Life

The fabric of Cuban life has changed dramatically since 1959. Health care is free and national in scope. The main transmissible and contagious diseases have been eradicated. Infant mortality dropped from 46.7 per 1000 live births in 1969 to 13.3 per 1000 live births at the end of 1987 and life expectancy is now over 74 years. Cuba has a doctor for every 400 inhabitants and a dentist for every 1864. The community doctor program first introduced in urban neighborhoods has been extended into the rugged Sierra Maestra and Escambray Mountains to provide closer medical liaison with rural residents. By the year 2000, Cuba expects to have 20,000 doctors in local consultation offices to cover the health care needs of the country.

As for diet, the per capita daily consumption stands at 2967 caloric units and 79.9 grams of protein, considerably higher than in most underdeveloped countries. Moreover, basic foods such as meat, milk, rice, beans and sugar are rationed and government subsidized to ensure equal distribution at low prices. Eggs, butter, bread, and fresh fruits and vegetables in season are unrationed, plentiful and cheap.

Education — which is completely free from elementary school through the university and cumpulsory through the ninth grade — is based on the concept of work and study. Modern high schools in the countryside combine agricultural and classroom activities, providing students with free educational materials, uniforms, room and board. Day students at city junior and senior high schools spend a month out of the school year working in the countryside. Some 90,000 toddlers — children of working mothers — attend nursery schools that charge a modest fee based on family income and number of children. In adult education, the goal is now completion of the ninth grade in the Workers and Farmers Education Program (EOC). More than three million Cubans out of a population of ten million are enrolled in some educational program.

Sports and Culture

Closely linked to both health and education is the emphasis on sports and recreation in Cuba. Baseball is as much the national sport of Cuba as of the United States — Cuban repatriates from the north brought the game back with them and contributed the proceeds from their exhibit matches to the 1895 War of Independence. In boxing, Cuba has champions in every weight category. Olympic and Pan American championships in volleyball, basketball, track and field and other sports that past Cuban athletes never practiced are the logical culmination of a massive sports program that reaches the entire population. Cuba will host the Pan American games in 1991 — new facilities for athletes and spectators are under construction — but sports are also viewed as an integral part of the education program and a key factor in preventive medicine. Indeed, the battle against sedentarism has won more converts than the anti-smoking campaign and Cubans of all ages now run and exercise in parks and gyms and along Havana's seaside Malecón.

Music, especially Afro-Cuban music, is the rhythmic base of Cubans' recreation and culture. Cuba is the home of the *son*, the cha-cha and especially the rumba created by marginalized black urban dwellers in the 19th century and still going strong — side by side with fine hot jazz; the romantic ballads of the traditional guitar-playing *trova*; the poetic-political songs of the *Nueva trova*, created by Silvio Rodríguez, Pablo Milanés and other post-revolution musicians; and such popular musical groups as Los Irakere, Son 14 and Los Van Van.

Carnival in Cuba is a veritable Afro-Cuban explosion of music and dance, with street choruses and elaborate floats. In both Havana and Santiago de Cuba, the street dances or *comparsas* are the epitome of these festivities, dating back to the mid-19th century. Everybody comes out for Carnival to watch the parade, drink the foamy beer that flows from huge tanks, down a shot of rum, sample food from the street stands and join a conga line. Carnival is celebrated in July in Havana and Santiago de Cuba and International Carnival rocks Varadero throughout January. Some smaller cities, such as Remedios with its century-old *parrandas*, have their own traditional carnival-type celebrations.

Cubans also appreciate the classical music played by guitarist Leo Brouwer and the young pianist Jorge Prats; they fill the theater when Alicia Alonso's National Ballet Company is performing; they comment on the fresh virtuosity of the younger Camagüey Ballet; they admire the choreography and agility of the Modern Dance Company; and black Cubans especially relate to the National Folklore Group's Rumba Saturday held in its outdoor patio. These are the spectator aspects of the rhythm and movement that are as basic and essential to the average Cuban's life as breathing, eating and talking.

The plastic arts — and film — are second only to music in reflecting the Cuban society. In painting they range from Manuel Mendive's detailed primitives of Afro-Cuban symbology to the late René Portocarrero's beflowered women and Tomás Sánchez's liquid landscapes. Cuban posters, a graphic adjunct of the mass media, tell people at a glance about production and defense goals, social and cultural events and struggles in other countries; and many of the silk-screen posters designed to promote Cuban films and festivals are real works of art.

More than any other medium, Cuban films have succeeded in reflecting the realities and conflicts of Cuban society with creativity and humor: among them scores of documentaries by Santiago Alvarez and Luis Felipe Bernaza and features that go back to Tomás Gutiérrez Alea's *Memories of Underdevelopment* in the early '60s, Juan Pablo Tabío's ironic commentary on the housing problem in *Se Permuta* (House Hunting) of the early 80s and Manuel Octavio Gómez's more recent *Patakín*, an uproarious paen to sugar production.

The annual New Latin-American Film Festival sponsored by the Cuban Institute of Cinematography (ICAIC) is an important event and its Coral prizes are the Oscars of Latin America.

The first film school in Latin America opened in Havana in 1987 under the direction of Argentine cinema director Fernando Birri. There, students from several Latin-American and African countries are studying the history and technique of film making for future application in their own countries.

Like films, Cuban theater often deals with social issues. The Escambray Theater Group, up in Cuba's central mountains, bases many of its scripts and acting on exchanges with the rural residents who are also its audience. Theater and musical groups are booked into provincial cities and also into outlying areas where they may perform in an open field.

In addition, all the provinces publish their own newspapers and broadcast their own radio programs; and even the smaller cities have writers and artists clubs, museums, bookstores, theaters and movie houses. Published in Havana, *Granma* is the daily newspaper of the Communist Party (a weekly summary is published in English and French as well as Spanish). Other Havana dailies are *Juventud rebelde* and *Trabajadores*. The weekly *Cartelera* newssheet keeps people up to date on cultural happenings and a host of general and specialized magazines appear weekly, monthly and quarterly.

Radio Havana Cuba beams its shortwave programs in eight languages including English, while Radio Taíno, Cuba's AM tourism station, broadcasts in English from 3 to 5 p.m. daily at 1160 on the dial and can be picked up easily on any hotel or portable radio. Two national TV channels serve the island and closed circuit Sun Channel TV offers tourist information and films to guests staying in Havana, Holguín, Varadero and other resort hotels.

The Cuban People

A product of capitalist underdevelopment modified by the benign bureaucracy of tropical socialism, the Cuban people are a sometimes contradictory blend of highly individual yet recognizably national characteristics. Their Spanish is a unique staccato slur of accents and idioms that differ from that spoken anywhere else. Their gestures, too — the impertinent, attention-getting "psst," the questioning nose wrinkle and the go-away hand signal that really means come here — are ingrained Cubanisms; and even the *piropo* or street compliment has survived. Cuban women walk with a sinuous coquetry, the men with a certain bravado (*guapería* is the Spanish word) that indicates a surviving — and tolerated — machismo. Generous, outgoing and fun-loving, *cubanos* are also self-sacrificing, reserved and disciplined. Aware of the instability of consumer products, they will queue for anything whether they need it or not — and voice their justified complaints about price, quality and service. Patriotic and loyal to their leaders, they are also profound social critics whose penetrating black humor spares nobody and is the yeast for their buoyant optimism about the future.

Workers at May Day rally

GETTING TO KNOW CUBA BY SEEING IT

For most visitors to Cuba, the point of arrival is either Havana or Varadero Beach, which lie 140 km. (86.8 mi.) apart on the north coast of western Cuba. Santiago de Cuba and Holguín, respectively 967 km. (600 mi.) and 771 km. (478 mi.) east of Havana, are also points of increasing interest for visitors. International flights bring tourists directly to these cities (as well as several smaller ones) and national flights connect all of them with other points of interest.

No matter where you land, though, Havana (population two million) is the hub — with so much to see and do that each visitor has to decide what points of interest in the city and what excursions out of the city are feasible in a finite vacation schedule. Take it by areas, then: Old Havana, the most densely populated (112,000 residents) 100-block area on the island as well as the most visited because of its colonial fortresses, churches and mansions; new Havana, with its many government buildings, opulent houses (now used mainly as embassies, offices or schools) and hotels (most of them near the busy Rampa in Vedado, a few further west in Miramar); and the outskirts (beaches, parks and special points of interest).

HAVANA

OLD HAVANA

Although early records disappeared in a pirate raid, July 25, 1515, is believed to be the date on which Diego Velázquez, first Governor of the island, established the original villa of San Cristóbal de La Habana on the southern coast of

HAVANA

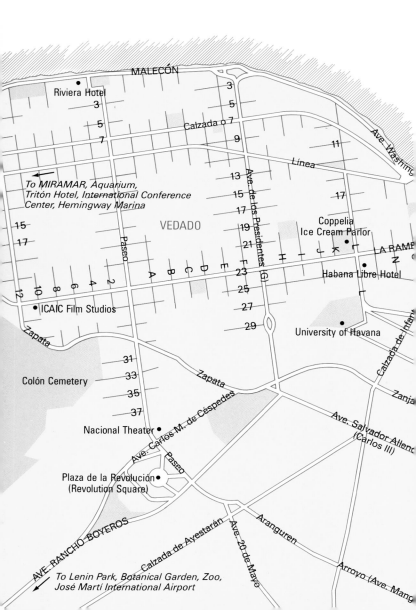

MALECÓN

Riviera Hotel

3

Calzada o 7

5

7

9

11

Línea

To MIRAMAR, Aquarium,
Tritón Hotel, International Conference
Center, Hemingway Marina

13

15

17

17

VEDADO

Coppelia
Ice Cream Parlor

15

19

17

21

LA RAMP

23

Habana Libre Hotel

25

ICAIC Film Studios

27

29

University of Havana

Zapata

31

33

Zapata

Colón Cemetery

35

37

Nacional Theater

Ave. Carlos M. de Céspedes

Ave. Salvador Allen
(Carlos III)

Zanja

Plaza de la Revolución
(Revolution Square)

Paseo

AVE. RANCHO BOYEROS

Calzada de Ayestarán

Ave. 20 de Mayo

Aranguren

Arroyo (Ave. Mang

To Lenin Park, Botanical Garden, Zoo,
José Martí International Airport

Ave. Washing

Ave. de los Presidentes (G)

Paseo

A B C D E

12 10 8 6 4 2

Zapata

Calzada de Infant

N

acional Hotel

25

Morro Castle

Ameijeras Hospital (MALECÓN) Ave. de Maceo

San Lázaro

CENTRAL
HAVANA

MALECÓN

La Punta Fortress

Neptuno

Deauville Hotel

(Ave. del Puerto) Carlos M. de Céspedes

San Rafael

Zanja

Paseo de Martí (PRADO)

Zulueta

Cuba

Tacón

Ave. de Italia (Galiano)

Belascoaín

Padre Varela

Museum of the Revolution
(Granma Memorial)

Empedrado

Ave. Simón Bolívar (Reina)

Inglaterra Hotel

García Lorca Theater

Capitol
(Academy of Sciences)

Parque Central
(Central Park)

Plaza de la Catedral
(Cathedral Square)

Obispo Plaza de Armas
(Arms Square)

Ave. de Bélgica

OLD HAVANA

Mercaderes

San Pedro

Indian Maiden Fountain

Máximo Gómez (Monte)

Muralla

Cienfuegos

Plaza de San Francisco
(San Francisco Square)

La Habana Indian settlement. The site was swampy and insalubrious, so the villa was transferred to the mouth of what is now the Almendares River, which proved equally unsatisfactory. Again the settlers packed up and moved to the port of Carenas, where they finally celebrated the founding of San Cristóbal de La Habana on November 16, 1519. The festivities allegedly took place under a leafy ceiba tree, at the spot where the shrine El Templete was subsequently built in Arms Square.

Havana quickly became a tumultuous, seaside city whose narrow streets accommodated the rich in their gigs and carriages, street vendors crying out their wares, burdened slaves and free blacks. The early huts made of wooden slabs and palm fronds were gradually replaced by modest stone houses and palatial mansions, great churches and convents and mighty defensive fortresses built between the 16th and 19th centuries.

Borrowing from the Moors, the colonists constructed their homes around central patios that were really lushly planted private parks, usually with wells and fountains. The great wooden portals on Havana mansions were designed to admit carriages so that merchandise could be conveniently unloaded and placed in the storerooms off the patio. A smaller door set in the portal admitted pedestrians. The ground floor rooms of the mansion were generally used for business and commerce. The slaves or servants were also quartered there or in the low-ceilinged *entresuelo*, a half floor between the storerooms and the mezzanine where the family lived. Opening off the balcony overlooking the patio, the family rooms were designed with marble floors, high ceilings and floor-to-ceiling louvered doors topped by stained-glass windows (*vitrales*, or more specifically *lucetas* if rectangular and *mediopuntos* if arched) — practical architectural devices used to keep them cool and ventilated and to filter the harsh tropical light.

Museum of the City, Arms Square

Arms Square

Plaza de las Armas (Arms Square) (*buses 27, 227, 82 or 98 from Vedado going east*), constructed alongside the port, was Havana's original center of political and military power. In the early 16th century it was called Church Square because the city's first parish church was built there. It became known as Arms Square after the troops quartered in La Real Fuerza Castle began to drill in it.

In the middle of the Square is a shady park with a statue of independence leader Carlos Manuel de Céspedes at its center. The "father of the country," as Céspedes is called, stands with his back to the **Palace of the Captains General** — now the **Museum of the City of Havana** and the city historian's office — seat of the colonial government from 1792, when it was completed, until 1898, when Spain withdrew from the island; and, beginning in 1902, offices of the first three presidents of the Republic.

Built on the site of Havana's first church, its interior patio contains Cuba's oldest monument, a tablet with a cross and an angel's head carved in relief, at the spot where a local noblewoman, Dona María de Cepero y Nieto, fell mortally wounded by a random shot from a harquebus in

1557 while saying her prayers in the chapel. In the center of the patio, royal palm trees tower over a white marble statue of Christopher Columbus and the cannon fired in colonial times to announce the closing of the city gates. (Ever since La Cabaña Fortress was completed in 1774, the traditional 9 p.m. cannon shot has been fired from its parapets on the far side of the harbor next to the Morro Castle.)

Designed by Antonio Fernández de Trevejos y Zaldívar, the Palace occupies the entire block bound by Obispo, Mercaderes and O'Reilly Streets. Its facade, facing Arms Square, has nine arcades supported by ten ionic columns crowned with the Spanish coat of arms carved in Italian marble by Giuseppe Gaggini. Great blocks of conchiferous rock were used in the exterior walls. The design of the Palace greatly influenced other structures of the period, so that many of Havana's colonial houses have moldings, cornices and other decorations similar to those first used in this building.

The museum's exhibits offer a sweeping view of Cuban history through gigs and carriages, paintings, documents, statues, furniture, household utensils, uniforms, flags and machetes used by famous Cuban independence fighters. The museum is also the permanent home of the original **La Giraldilla** — the graceful bronze weathervane in the form of a woman holding the Cross of Calatrava in her left hand, created by sculptor Jerónimo Martín Pinzón and cast in his Havana foundry sometime between 1630 and 1634.

The figure represents Doña Inés de Bobadilla, Cuba's first woman governor, who replaced her husband Hernando de Soto when he left Cuba to conquer Florida in 1539. According to legend, Doña Inés was frequently seen gazing out to sea searching the horizon for the ship that would bring her husband home; but De Soto died on the banks of the Mississippi River in 1542.

For many years, La Giraldilla pirouetted atop the tower of La Real Fuerza Castle. After being blown down in a hurricane, however, the original figure was replaced by a replica. La Giraldilla has become a symbol of Havana and, in-

La Giraldilla
weathervane

deed, of Cuba, for her image also circles the globe on the label of the island's best-known export rum, Havana Club.

The Museum of the City of Havana is open Tuesday through Saturday from 2:30 to 6 and 7 to 10 p.m. and Sunday from 9 a.m. to 1 p.m. Tel.: 61-0722.

Next to it on the north side of the Square is the former **Intendencia Palace**, where two publishing houses have their offices.

In 1538 — shortly after the catastrophic pirate attack that reduced Havana to ashes — Governor Hernando de Soto ordered construction of a fortress that would protect the city. **La Real Fuerza Castle**, Cuba's oldest, was completed in 1545 under the direction of Captain Mateo Aceituno. For centuries the fortress guarded the portside entrance to Arms Square, its moat and drawbridge facing seaward. It is now the **Arms Museum**, *open Monday and Wednesday through Saturday from 11 a.m. to 6:45 p.m. and Sunday from 8 a.m. to 12:45 p.m. Tel.: 80-0216.*

At the northeast corner of Arms Square, the neoclassic **El Templete** (erected in 1827) and its symbolic ceiba tree (a replacement of the original) mark the city's founding. Inside El Templete are three murals painted by French artist Jean Baptiste Vermay, who is buried below his work. One mural depicts the first mass and another the first Town Council meeting, while the third represents the inauguration of El Templete, showing the figures who were present.

El Templete's present ceiba tree was planted early in 1959. Like all ceibas, this one is believed to have magical powers and, when the city's founding is commemorated on November 16, those who attend the festivities observe the tradition of walking around the tree three times as they make a wish.

Next to El Templete, at No. 1 Baratillo Street, is the early-19th-century palace built for the *Count de Santovenia*, who in 1833, hosted the bash of the century there, a three-day affair climaxed by the ascent from the rooftop of a gas-filled balloon whose passengers rose in a basket decorated with flowers, ribbons and streamers. After the flamboyant Count's death in 1865, a New Orleans colonel bought the place and turned it into the Santa Isabel Hotel. US writer Samuel Hazard stayed there in 1868 and, in his book *Cuba with Pen and Pencil*, praised its food and service, its English-speaking staff that included chambermaids (then unknown in Cuba) and its proximity to the US Embassy.

On the ground floor of the mansion — where the Count stored fish and oil — the enticing smell of smoked sausages, meat pies and Spanish turnovers now wafts from a colonial-style tavern called *Mesón de la Flota* (Fleet's Inn); and above the tavern is a boutique and its collateral artisans' workshop. The building is being reconverted into an urban inn, retaining the colonial features that make it such a harmonious part of Arms Square.

Off Arms Square

A block further along Baratillo Street, at Jústiz, is the patio theater of the *House of Comedy*, headquarters of the Anaquillé Theater Group whose offices are in the former slave quarters owned by the Marquis de Jústiz. The group performs children's plays and comedies in the patio and experimental works in its smaller, inside studio.

Jústiz is a block-long street that ends at Oficios, where the *Automobile Museum* exhibits old cars — nothing like the variety of smoothly running Chevrolets, Chryslers and Fords from the '50s (or older) you'll see on the streets, of course. Across Oficios Street is Monte Piedad, the city's first pawnshop and now the *Numismatic Museum* of the National Bank of Cuba. Next door is *Arabian House*, with its treasures from Arab countries and the delightfully intimate — as well as modestly priced — *Al Medina Restaurant*, which serves Arab specialties *(tel.: 61-8715 for reservations since space is limited)*. A few doors away is the *Cigar Salon* with its exhibits on the history of the world-famous Havana cigars that are hand-rolled in a variety of lengths and cir-cumferences and marketed under some 25 brand names.

A right turn onto Oficios Street takes you back into Arms Square at the corner of Obispo, site of the bishopric for which the street was named and Havana's first school for girls, San Francisco de Sales, founded in 1699 and open until 1925. One of the most picturesque streets in Old Havana, Obispo is a pedestrian throughway that runs straight through the old city to Floridita Restaurant — US writer Ernest Hemingway's favorite bar — at the corner of Monserrate Street.

It was on Obispo Street in Arms Square that colonial master silversmith Don Gregorio Tabares had his shop in one of Havana's earliest houses, now a silverware exhibit hall. And the charmingly restored commercial buildings overlooking the Square include the *Casa del Café con Leche*, *La Mina Bar-Restaurant* (specializing in Cuban dishes), an old-fashioned barbershop, *La Tinaja* (where you can drink clear water from a great ceramic water cooler), the *Casa de la Natilla* (which serves custards) and, at the corner of Mer-

Coffee, any time, any place

caderes, the *Santa Catalina French Pharmacy*, a museum and green-medicine shop that sells herbs and plants.

Directly behind the Museum of the City on the far side of Mercaderes Street is the jarringly modern building of the *Ministry of Education*, site of Havana's first university: the *Royal and Papal University of San Jerónimo*, founded January 5, 1768. The great bronze bell that used to call the students to class remains as a monument, though the University was transferred in 1902 to the new section of the city and rechristened the University of Havana.

At the corner of Obispo and Mercaderes is the *Ambos Mundos Hotel*, where Ernest Hemingway lived and wrote during his early days in Havana. It was from this modest hotel that he set out along Obispo Street for the port, where his yacht *Pilar* was docked; or, in the other direction, for Floridita Bar to enjoy his Daiquiri. Today the Ambos Mundos Hotel — except for Hemingway's room, which is kept as a museum — is used to house teachers and administrators who come to Havana from other parts of the country for educational meetings and seminars.

Turning left on Mercaderes past the green-medicine pharmacy, you come to the *Casa de las Infusiones* (House of Brews), which offers hot and cold drinks made with aromatic and medicinal plants: chamomile, vanilla, tea, sweet basil, oregano, linden, anise and, of course, sweet fragrant Cuban coffee.

A few yards beyond is *La Torre de Marfil* (Ivory Tower) *Restaurant*, specializing in oriental food. At the corner of Mercaderes and Obrapía Streets is the *Benito Juárez Cuba-Mexico Friendship House*, containing photos, documents and other materials pertaining to Mexican history and culture.

On Obrapía Street (a right turn off Mercaderes), in a spacious 19th-century building, is *Africa House*, which offers a general panorama of Africa's many cultures in exhibits of musical instruments, jewelry, clothing, objects of the Yoruba tribes (that had such an influence on Cuban history) weapons, furniture, sculpture and the fabulous gifts that African leaders have bestowed on Cuban President

Fidel Castro. The museum also contains ethnologist Fernando Ortiz's important Afro-Cuban collection.

Across from Africa House, a great mansion with a sober facade occupies more than half a block: *Obra Pía House*, for which the street is named, now functions as a protocol house for the mayor of the city. In the 17th century, the original dwelling was remodeled with the addition of adjacent buildings to care for five orphans a year with a stipend of 102,000 pesos provided by the owner-benefactor Captain Calvo de la Puerta. The great portal was made in Spain and shipped to Havana.

At the corner of Obrapía and San Ignacio Streets stands the former home of Gaspar Riberos de Vasconcelos, 17th-century knight of the Order of Christ, the emblem displayed at the entrance. The mansion is now the *Arts and Crafts Center of the Federation of Cuban Women*.

Old Square

A left turn onto San Ignacio Street leads to **Plaza Vieja (Old Square)** five blocks away, which became the focal point of urban commercial and social life after Arms Square was taken over for military drills and troop assemblies. The most luxurious building on this square is the former Count de Jaruco's mansion, with its great entrance door and glowing stained-glass arches covering the entire front of the second story. Now the **Fondo de Bienes Culturales (Foundation for Cultural Assets)**, it programs auctions, sales, fashion shows, meetings with artists and musical entertainment. *Open Monday through Saturday from 9 a.m. to 8 p.m. Tel.: 61-3503.*

At San Ignacio and Sol Streets, a right turn takes you to the **Santa Clara Convent** at the corner of Cuba. Built between 1638 and 1643, this walled religious city is now being restored and one cloister of the 1.2-hectare complex has already been completed to house the **National Center of Conservation, Restoration and Museums**.

A few blocks on, at Cuba and Jesús María, is the **Espíritu Santo Church,** built in 1632. The oldest church in Cuba and the only one with catacombs, it was reopened in 1987 after extensive restoration.

Cuba Street ends at Ave. del Puerto and the ruins of *Paula Church*. Just to the west is the seaside *Alameda de Paula*, where the marble walk and iron street lamps of Havana's first promenade are completely overshadowed by docks, warehouses, stores and bars that show the more commercial and seamier side of the waterfront. Further along, across from the Customs House, is **San Francisco Convent and Square**. Because of its proximity to the port, the square was a busy commercial center in colonial days. Today, the cartons and containers unloaded on the docks across from it are trucked directly to their final destination. San Francisco Square is deserted except for the **Fountain of Lions**, Italian sculptor Gaggini's playful complement to the austere facade of San Francisco Convent (1584). On a hot day, the convent's leafy patio and its air-duct cooling system devised by colonial architects make it a welcome haven.

Fountain of Lions

Cathedral of Havana

Cathedral Square

Of all Havana's many squares, the most harmonious in terms of its architecture is **Plaza de la Catedral (Cathedral Square)** — a block west of Arms Square on Mercaderes or San Ignacio Streets.

Entering the square from San Ignacio Street, the baroque **Cathedral of Havana** looms ahead. On the left is Chorro

Alley and the plaque marking the outlet for Havana's first aqueduct, the Zanja Real. The plaque is affixed to what used to be a bath house and is now the *Cathedral Square Gallery*, which sells arts and crafts, records and books.

Next to it is the former mansion of the Marquis de Aguas Claras, now *El Patio Restaurant*: terrace overlooking the square, central dining patio with plashing fountain, long mahogany bar on one side and enclosed dining rooms on the other. *Snacks are served on the terrace and meals can be ordered in the restaurant from noon to 1 a.m. (average price per meal about $8). Tel.: 62-1447.*

Directly across the square from the Patio Restaurant is the former Lombillo mansion, opened as the *Education Museum (Tel.: 61-9386)* in January 1987 after a two-year restoration. Built in 1587 as a tile kiln and residence, it was the home of the wealthy Pedrosa family for over a hundred years and then of the Lombillos until the end of the 19th century, when it was sold for residential-commercial use. For many years, La Cueva Tavern operated in the corner room, now devoted to internationalist teachers. The exhibits are displayed in white-walled rooms with blue-beamed ceilings and floors laid with five-sided red tiles duplicated from the originals found on the mezzanine. There visitors learn about the all-out literacy campaign of 1961 when more than 700,000 people out of a population of seven million were taught to read and write by young teachers who went into rural areas with their notebooks and enthusiasm to make the island a "territory free of illiteracy." Another room is devoted to the early greats of Cuban education, and still another to José Martí's teachings and writings.

Next to the Education Museum and sharing the same colonnade is the Peñalver mansion where the artists of the *Experimental Graphics Workshop* produce prints and posters while visitors watch. The graphics can also be purchased.

Opposite the Cathedral is the palace of the Count de Bayona, now the **Museum of Colonial Art** *(Tel.: 61-1367)* which exhibits colonial furniture, lamps, porcelain and other ornamental objects. The stained glass collection is a

Stained glass *mediopuntos*, Museum of Colonial Art, Cathedral Square

marvel of pink roses, purple tulips, crimson suns with golden rays, white wheels entwined with green vines and every imaginable combination of geometric patterns — all demonstrating the eminently secular concept and application of stained glass in Cuba.

Dominating the square is the limestone **Cathedral**, with its unmatched bell towers and sculptured facade. It was built in stages by unknown craftsmen and finally completed around 1777.

The Jesuit fathers had a chapel on the site in 1741, when a bolt of lightning struck the ship **Invincible** in Havana harbor and sent part of its rigging into Arms Square, destroying the parochial church there. Whatever religious objects could be saved from the ruins were transferred for safekeeping to the San Ignacio Chapel, which was enlarged with a church and monastery. After the Jesuits were expelled from Cuba in 1767, Havana became the island's eastern diocese and San Ignacio was consecrated as the Cathedral of Havana on November 24, 1789.

The Cathedral's interior forms a rectangle 103 feet wide and 180 feet long divided into three naves separated by great columns. Each of the side naves has four chapels while the main altar is in the center of the apse.

For a time, the urn allegedly bearing the remains of Admiral Christopher Columbus was safeguarded in a Cathedral vault, having been transferred to Cuba from the Dominican Republic when that country gained its freedom from Spain. In 1898, just before Spain withdrew from Cuba, the urn was sent to Seville. But even today, the claim is made that Columbus' remains never really left the Dominican Republic.

Regular services are held in the Cathedral and a guided tour is offered on Saturday afternoons — a good time to visit Cathedral Square for the weekly arts and crafts sale and entertainment by musicians, dancers, or puppeteers.

Facing the harbor behind the Cathedral is the *San Carlos Seminary*, which has been training philosophers, theologians and priests since 1772. Father Félix Varela developed his anti-colonial philosophy as an early 19th-century teacher in its halls. Nineteenth-century novelist Cirilo Villaverde was a lay student there — like Leonardo, the hero of his famous novel *Cecilia Valdés*, who also knew the seminary's refreshing interior patio and great stone staircase.

A few steps beyond Cathedral Square on Empedrado Street is *La Bodeguita del Medio Restaurant* — literally, the little store in the middle of the block, which is how it started. This popular hole-in-the-wall was originally a hangout for bohemian artists who appreciated its good food and informal atmosphere. Today the Bodeguita is everybody's favorite and anyone can add to the graffiti decor. The cooking is typically Cuban (roast pork is the specialty) and savory aromas perfume the air as you sip a refreshing Mojito — Havana Club rum and soda poured over a base of lime juice, crushed mint and sugar and decorated with a sprig of mint — before your meal (average price per person $12 with two beers).

The Bodeguita is open from noon to 4 p.m. and 6:30 p.m. to 1:30 a.m. Reservations are a must. Tel.: 6-6120 or request them through your hotel tourism bureau.

Near Cathedral Square, at the intersection of Tacón, Cuba and Chacón Streets, is an open excavation that reveals a part of Old Havana's colonial past: the *Artillery Sentry Box*, walls and passages of the old San Telmo Barracks overlooking the port.

Next to this excavation is the *Old Havana Amphitheater*, where musical groups and individual artists perform at evening and weekend concerts.

Across from the Amphitheater is the **Palacio de Artesanía Cubana (Palace of Cuban Arts and Crafts)** in a recently restored colonial mansion built in 1780. A number of craft workshops operate on the upper floors and the shops sell fashions by designer Lina, records and musical instruments, leather goods, jewelry, ceramics, dolls, hats, silk-screen prints, woven fiber goods and — of course — Cuban rum and Havana cigars.

A block west, at the intersection of Espada and Aguiar Streets, is the *Music Museum*, which traces the history of Cuban music and musical instruments.

Presidential Palace and Angel Hill

Behind the Music Museum, the broad Ave. de las Misiones (Monserrate) leads up from the statue of *Máximo Gómez* to the former **Presidential Palace**, now the **Museum of the Revolution**.

The history of the Presidential Palace is intimately linked to corruption and oppression by the Cuban presidents who made it their headquarters before the triumph of the revolution in 1959. A commando of the Revolutionary Student Directorate attacked the Presidential Palace on March 13, 1957, in a thwarted attempt to assassinate dictator Fulgencio Batista. The delivery truck they used to enter the premises is on display at the point where the young rebels dismounted and rushed up the back stairway to Batista's private office. The dictator escaped and most of the rebels were killed by guards inside the palace. The Museum's exhibits — photos, documents, diagrams, a model of the Moncada Garrison and personal objects used by the guerrillas — trace Cuba's turbulent history in enlightening detail. *Open Tuesday through Sunday from 10 a.m. to 6 p.m. Tel.: 61-5307, 6-8849, 6-9210 and 61-6971.*

In back of the Museum of the Revolution is the **Granma** cabin cruiser in which Fidel and his followers returned from exile in Mexico on December 2, 1956, to begin fighting in the Sierra Maestra Mountains. The *Granma* floats on a simulated sea inside an air-conditioned, glass-enclosed "harbor." Surrounding it are planes, tanks and other vehicles related to the struggle.

From Monserrate Street, the **Santo Angel Custodio Church** seems to be built into the rock of **Angel Hill,** while its cream-colored bell tower and a dozen slender Gothic spires soar from the summit into the pale blue sky. At the foot of the hill, 23 wide stone steps lead up to the rear door beside the altar, but the main entrance is on Compostela Street, named for the bishop who built the church in 1689.

There in the square, facing the lofty church portals, is a bust of the man who immortalized Angel Hill in his palpably real characterization of Cuban life in the 1820s. The inscription reads:

> Cirilo Villaverde, 1812-1894, Cuba's most famous novelist, fervent patriot and revolutionary who suffered prison and exile for the freedom of Cuba. With Angel Hill as the setting, his creative genius gave birth to *Cecilia Valdés*, admirable novel of 19th-century manners.

Villaverde's protagonists are Cecilia Valdes — a beautiful headstrong mulatto — and Leonardo Gamboa — the indolent son of a wealthy slave trader — whose incestuous passion is doomed from the start. But before the melodramatically violent denouement takes place on the steps of Santo Angel Custodio Church, Villaverde paints in compelling detail the brutality, hypocrisy and vulgarity of the colonial ruling class and the smouldering resentment of the oppressed blacks.

Yet the idea of freedom — from the slave master, from Spanish domination — was germinating, even though the liberation philosophy of Father Félix Varela — who was baptized in Santo Angel Custodio Church on November 27, 1788 — was suppressed and the illustrious Cuban thinker exiled during the period of Villaverde's novel.

Sixty-five years after that baptism, José Martí, the man who brought Varela's liberation philosophy to fruition, was also baptized in Santo Angel Church — an event commemorated by a bronze plaque on the church facade.

In the period between those prophetic baptisms, the single-towered baroque church changed little. Then, in 1860, the present black-and-white marble floor was laid; and in 1868, under the direction of Fray Jacinto María Martínez, extensive remodeling and expansion was begun. The neo-Gothic steeples that so distinguish the exterior were added, as well as the carved mahogany altars with their matching Gothic spires. The existing organ was installed in 1869 and the church was reopened in 1870. The side chapel was constructed in 1894 and the only additions after that were the Monserrate entrance and the precious stained glass windows imported from Barcelona and Munich in 1923. All these features were enhanced by the restoration completed in 1986. The church has daily services and baptisms as requested.

It's easy to imagine this as the church of the aristocracy, not only in the 1820s before it was remodeled, but in the 1920s after the luxurious Presidential Palace was built just a few feet away. In both periods, it would also have been the setting for such splendid weddings as the one between Leonardo Gamboa and Isabel Ilincheta, approved by both families.

But Leonardo's rival for Cecilia Valdés, a mulatto like Cecilia, frustrated the culmination of those nuptial vows by stabbing Leonardo to death at the portals of Santo Angel Custodio Church, that evocative architectural, historical, religious and literary landmark on Angel Hill in Old Havana.

Museum of Fine Arts

On the south side of the **Granma** memorial, where Trocadero Street crosses Monserrate, is the modern **National
Museum of Fine Arts**, which contains a representative collection of Cuban paintings and sculpture as well as examples of European and Egyptian art. In addition to its
exhibits, the Museum of Fine Arts has a full program of
conferences, films and musical presentations. *The museum
is open Tuesday through Sunday from 2 to 8:30 p.m. Tel.: 6-
8198.*

On the other corner of Trocadero is the delightfully old-
fashioned *Sevilla Hotel*, scene of the comical intrigue in
Graham Greene's *Our Man in Havana.* The Sevilla is one of
the many Havana hotels scheduled for restoration by 1990.

*To reach this area directly from the Vedado or Miramar neigh-
borhoods, take bus 22, 27, 64, 67, 82, l32 or 227 to Central Park
and walk a block east.*

Near Central Park

At Monserrate between O'Reilly and Obispo Streets is a
small park containing a statue of Francisco de Albear, who
engineered Havana's first modern water drainage system
in the late 19th century. Facing the park on Obispo Street
are *La Moderna Poesía Bookstore*, Havana's largest, and
Floridita Restaurant. **La Zaragozana Restaurant** is right
around the corner on Monserrate. The two restaurants are
among Havana's best and both are expensive: average
price $20 per person without drinks.

Two famous names are intimately associated with
Floridita: bartender Constante, who created the Daiquiri;
and writer Ernest Hemingway, who praised its creation
with frequent visits to the bar and immortalized the drink
in his *Islands in the Stream.* Noted for its fine seafood,
Floridita is open from noon to midnight. *Tel.: 6l-0806 for reservations or make them through the hotel tourism bureau.*

La Zaragozana serves more than 150 dishes from
Spanish, Cuban and international cuisines, specializing in
seafood. Seating is in order of arrival.

Just beyond La Zaragozana is Lamparilla Street, where Greene's vacuum cleaner salesman-agent and his wayward daughter Millie lived at No. 37 (it doesn't exist). From Lamparilla, you can turn right on Bernaza Street and walk a block to Christ Square and *Santo Cristo del Buen Viaje Church*. At one corner of the square is the 300-year-old Grapevine House, which has recently been restored as the *Vietnamese Friendship House*.

Continuing on Bernaza past the Grapevine House, you emerge on Monserrate, now Egido Street. Six blocks ahead is the **José Martí Museum**, at the corner of Leonor Pérez Street (named for Martí's mother), across from the railroad terminal.

The house in which Cuban patriot and intellectual José Martí was born on January 28, 1853, displays letters, documents and articles written by him and photos and objects relating to the varied aspects of his fruitful life. *Open Tuesday through Saturday from 11 a.m. to 7 p.m. and Sunday from 9 a.m. to 1 p.m. Tel.: 6-8852.*

In front of the railroad terminal on the west side of Egido Street is a guard post and a section of the *Old City Wall* that once enclosed Havana. That tremendous construction job designed to defend the capital from pirate attacks began in 1663 and was finally completed in 1740 at a cost of three million pesos. Improved, changed and adapted by various colonial governments, the wall eventually became a hindrance to the city's growth and a dubious means of defense — as was proven when the British seized Havana. In 1863, permission was finally granted to demolish it.

Prado Promenade

From the terminal, Zulueta Street leads north to the corner of Monte, where a left turn and a one-block walk brings you to the southern end of **Paseo de Martí (Prado)**. Here, at the corner of Monte and Cárdenas Streets, is the *Abel Santamaría* International Bookstore, which stocks a wide selection of books in foreign languages (English, French, German and Russian), published mainly in Cuba and the Soviet Union.

Walking down the Prado, on the left, you pass *Fraternity Park*, shaded by a spreading ceiba tree planted in soil brought from all the countries of the Americas on the occasion of the sixth Pan American Conference held in 1928.

Overlooking the park is the neoclassical Aldama Palace, considered one of Havana's three most important 19th-century mansions. It was originally the home of wealthy patriot Miguel Aldama, who was forced to flee the country when Spanish Volunteers sacked the place after the outbreak of the 1868 War of Independence. For years after that war, the sumptuous salons in the mansion were used as storerooms and offices, complicating the restoration work which was recently completed. The Aldama Palace is now headquarters for the *Institute of the History of the Communist Movement and the Socialist Revolution.*

In the center of the Prado stands Gaggini's white Carrara marble *Indian Maiden Fountain*, often referred to as Noble Havana — an appealing figure with a Greek profile and a feathered headdress. To the west, on Dragones Street, is the *José Martí Theater*, where the Constitutional Convention met in 1900.

Prado Promenade

The most prominent building on the Prado is the former **Capitol** — an excellent copy of Washington's — which now houses the **Academy of Sciences** and the **Felipe Poey Museum of Natural Sciences**. On either side of its main portal are sculptures representing Labor and Virtue, while the monumental marble statue symbolizing the Republic — now inclining dangerously to the right and surrounded by protective scaffolding until she can be repaired — dominates the domed lobby.

A block beyond is the **Great Theater of Havana** (which most Cubans still refer to as the **García Lorca**. Completed in 1837, the theater is still a glittering setting for seasonal performances by the National Ballet, Opera and Light Opera Companies.

At the corner of the San Rafael Mall — where you'll run into half of Havana on any shopping afternoon — is the *Inglaterra Hotel*, Cuba's finest when it was built in the 1880s and now Havana's oldest operating hotel (84 rooms with private baths and telephones).

General Antonio Maceo stayed there in February of 1890 when he came to Havana to sound out liberationist sentiments during the hiatus in Cuba's Wars of Independence. Maceo was a hero to the young independence sympathizers who hung out in front of the hotel on the *Louvre sidewalk* (named for the café next to the hotel, where there's now a pizzeria) and some 200 of them followed him into battle when the war was resumed in 1895. The plaque outside the hotel entrance lists the names of the "lads of the Louvre sidewalk" who died for Cuba's independence. The Inglaterra overlooks *Central Park*, with its marble fountains and shaded benches surrounding a central statue of José Martí.

Late in the afternoon, when the sun hangs low on the horizon and the soft sea breeze blows in, people like to stroll on down the laurel-lined Prado Promenade with its friendly bronze lions, past apartment and office buildings, restaurants, shops and the ornate *Marriage Palace*, where most local weddings take place.

Malecón Seaside Drive and Morro Castle

Morro Castle and La Punta

At the foot of the Prado Promenade and start of the Malecón Seaside Drive is the **Monument to the Medical Students** executed in 1871, in front of **San Salvador de La Punta Fortress** on the shore. Directly across the harbor is **Los Tres Reyes del Morro Castle**. Both fortresses were designed by Italian engineer Juan Bautista Antonelli, who was also the architect for the Morro Castle of Santiago de Cuba.

French explorer Samuel de Champlain, who visited Havana in 1601, wrote of the two new fortresses connected by an iron chain across the entrance to the port, noting that the Morro was garrisoned with 400 soldiers and La Punta with 200.

Havana's defenses proved adequate for more than a century, until British forces seized the city in 1762, holding it for nearly a year until it was returned to Spain in exchange for the Florida Peninsula. After the British departed, Spanish engineer Silvestre Abarca designed the more modern *La Cabaña Fortress*, behind the Morro, which took 11 years to complete. Next to the Morro stands the lighthouse that has guided so many seamen to safe harbor since it was built in 1845.

The Morro is now an atmospheric relic of the past, with a cool tavern and a great view of the city skyline. La Cabaña, which was still a military stronghold when Che seized it in 1959, is now in the process of restoration. *Both can be reached by car or by buses 58, 65, 162, 195, 204 or 216 from La Punta Park through the tunnel and also aboard the sailing ship* Fénix.

Across the Bay

For another view of the city, take the ferry from the Havana docks across the bay to **Casablanca** or **Regla**. The Casablanca ferry leaves from Caballería Dock and the Regla ferry from Luz Dock, both on Ave. del Puerto. Caballería is directly in front of Arms Square and Luz is opposite Los Marinos Bar at the corner of San Pedro and Santa Clara Streets. The one-way trip costs ten centavos.

Brightly painted houses climb the Casablanca hillside toward an immanent stone Christ and the domed National Observatory at the top. From Casablanca, an electric trolley

Regla, across the bay by ferry

train toots off on a three-hour trip to the city of *Matanzas*, stopping at 45 towns and villages along the way. The *tranvía,* as Cubans call it, was built in 1918 to connect the big *Hershey* (now *Camilo Cienfuegos) Sugarmill* with the two nearest port cities and the canefield outposts in between. The little wooden cars (said to be the originals) are as picturesque as the countryside they go through and the passengers are, for the most part, regular commuters: field hands dressed in baggy pants, long-sleeved shirts and straw hats; truck and tractor drivers in work clothes;

women carrying small children and huge shopping bags; teen-agers dressed for the beach. The fare to Matanzas is $1.03 with reserved seat. The ride, combined with a tour of the city, is a delightful half day's excursion en route to Varadero Beach, 35 km. (22 mi.) east of Matanzas by bus (50 centavos) or taxi ($4).

Regla celebrated its 300th birthday in 1987 with the completion of such important restorations as the main square and the *Santísima Virgen de Regla Church*. The wooden image of the black Virgin of Regla holding a white baby was copied from a fifth century African sculpture and has been in the church since 1696. She is considered patron and protector of sailors, the Catholic counterpart of Yemayá, African goddess of the sea and deep water in the Yoruba religion. Catholic mass and Yoruba rituals are both celebrated on September 8, day of the Virgin of Regla. The church has daily services at 8 and 9 a.m. and special services on the 8th of every month. Saints' images, rosaries and other ritualistic accessories can be acquired in the church.

Regla is also a working-class town with a long history of struggle commemorated on *Lenin Hill (bus number 29 from the ferry)*. When Lenin died, the residents of Regla held a public meeting and planted an olive tree there in his honor. The tree was uprooted by repressive forces then and on several subsequent occasions, but the defiant citizens of Regla always planted another. Now Lenin's profile is carved into the slope where an olive tree planted in 1959 grows next to the Lenin Nursery School. At the top of the hill — with the bay and the city of Havana laid out before you — is the Regla Municipal Museum which documents the revolutionary history of the little town.

NEW HAVANA

In Havana, all roads lead to the *Malecón*, that splendid drive and promenade that mediates between the city and the sea. Highrise apartment and office buildings, hotels, playgrounds, parks and ancient fortresses overlook the

Malecón; and beyond its broad wall, the rippling water — sometimes gray, sometimes blue, often crowned with whitecaps — cradles ships flying the flags of the world.

Drivers speed along the Malecón's six-lane highway while patient fishermen spend hours with their backs to the traffic. Early morning joggers trot along the wide esplanade. Children laugh and play on the seawall, lovers make it their trysting place, teen-agers swim below it. And sunset on the Malecón is everyone's favorite image.

In July, the Malecón becomes an enormous theater under the sky. Dazzling floats, brilliantly costumed street dancers and rhythmic musicians parade in that explosion called *Carnival.* All Havana turns out for it, lining up at the kiosks for a tasty tamale and a big foamy beer, dancing in the streets, singing with friends . . . letting loose.

The Malecón runs from La Punta Castle at the foot of the Prado westward to La Chorrera (a 17th-century fortress with a tavern in its tower) and the opulent *1830 Restaurant (excellent international cuisine at about $15 per person; tel.: 3-5230 for reservations).*

Overlooking the Malecón at the corner of Galiano, in Central Havana's busy commercial district, is the three-star *Deauville Hotel* (double rooms from $35 to $45, restaurant, bar, shops and rooftop pool). Further west the modern *Ameijeiras Hospital* — Havana's biggest and newest health care complex — rises behind *Maceo Park,* where kids play ball under the mounted figure of General Antonio Maceo wielding his machete.

La Rampa

Roughly at its half point, the Malecón is intersected by 23rd Street, whose five blocks up the hill to L Street are known as *La Rampa*, the city's busy nerve center. Ministries, airlines, travel agencies, banks, restaurants, cabarets, stores and movie houses line the Rampa, which ends where the towering *Habana Libre Hotel* (the city's largest, its air-conditioned double rooms with private baths range from $49 to $92 a night and it also has several restaurants, bars and shops and an outdoor pool) overlooks the white-domed

Coppelia Ice Cream Parlor — try one of the exotic tropical fruit flavors.

Near the Rampa are the three-star *Colina, St. John's* and *Vedado Hotels* (air-conditioned double rooms with private baths from $27 to $34) and the four-star gilt-and-marble *Capri*, old-world *Nacional* and exquisitely small and select *Victoria Hotels* (air-conditioned double rooms with private baths from $45 to $59). All have their own restaurants, shops and tourism bureaus. The Vedado, Capri and Victoria have a pool each and the Nacional has two, as well as a tennis court and extensive gardens.

From the Nacional's hilltop location, guests can glance westward along the Malecón for a view of the monument commemorating the sinking of the **USS Maine** in Havana harbor — the pretext for the Spanish-American War. The chain and anchor at the base of the monument were rescued from the battleship. The iron and bronze eagle that once topped the monument was toppled after the triumph of the revolution when Cubans became exasperated at US hostility toward their government. The broken eagle is on display on the first loggia of the Museum of the City, in Arms Square.

The Rampa undoubtedly has more good restaurants than any other area in Havana. In the lower lobby of the Havana Libre Hotel is *El Polinesio, tel.: 32-3753,* specializing in Polynesian barbecued chicken (average price $15 per person). In front of the Nacional is *Monseigneur, tel.: 32-9884*, which offers an international cuisine (average price $15 per person). In the Focsa Building at M and 17th Streets are *El Emperador* on the ground floor, *tel.: 32-4998,* international cuisine at an average of $20 per person; and *La Torre* at the top, *tel.: 32-4630,* where you can enjoy excellent food and a magnificent view of the city (average price $15 per person). Across from the Focsa on M Street is *El Conejito, tel.: 70-5502,* specializing in rabbit (average price $15 per person).

Tropicana Nightclub

There are bars and cabarets aplenty around the Rampa and the big hotels have nightly musical shows. But by far the best show in town is at famous **Tropicana Nightclub** *(72 Street between 43 and Línea, out of the center city, so make reservations for dinner, show and transportation through the hotel tourism bureau).* Tropicana is a myth, a fantasy of the '50s, a spellbinding kaleidoscope that's not to be missed. At the entrance to the nightclub, a stylized ballerina created by Cuban sculptor Rita Longo pirouettes in welcome. Along the driveway, colored lights play on royal palms, coconut, genip and mango trees. Centered in the walkway, the Dance of the Hours Fountain sprays a pastel mist. Guests pass through dazzling portals to an outdoor ballroom where trees reach toward a starry sky. This is the setting for drinks, dinner and the hour-and-a-half superproduction featuring a cast of more than 150, including a 32-piece orchestra.

Tropicana Nightclub Show

From La Rampa

After a night on the town have a look at the serious side of the city. Two blocks beyond the Habana Libre Hotel on L Street is the **University of Havana**. At the foot of the grand staircase — scene of so many student demonstrations — is the *Julio Antonio Mella Memorial*, honoring the popular student leader and founder of Cuba's first Communist Party who was gunned down by dictator Machado's hired thugs on the streets of Mexico City in 1929.

The *Montané Anthropological Museum* in the University Science Building contains an interesting collection of pre-Columbian Indian artifacts recovered from digs in several regions of Cuba. The neoclassic buildings around the campus quadrangle are still used for classes and academic meetings, but the University has spread all over the city to accommodate the constant jump in college enrollment as a result of Cuba's free educational system.

At 23rd and J Streets, diagonally across from Coppelia, is *Quixote Park*, where the sad-faced knight is mounted naked on his horse Rocinante, a free and unencumbered figure created in iron and wire by Sergio Martínez Sopena.

The *Cuban Institute of Cinematography (ICAIC)* and the *Charles Chaplin Theater*, where new Cuban films are often previewed, are located on 23rd between 10th and 12th Streets. Screenings can be arranged in ICAIC's studios. To get there, take any bus that stops on 23rd Street in front of Coppelia).

On the way, at 23rd and G Streets, the bus passes the *Castillo de Jagua Restaurant*, recommended for its shellfish specialties. Seating is in order of arrival and prices run around $20 per person.

To Revolution Square

Daytime sightseeing in modern Havana will surely include a visit to **Revolution Square** *(a five-minute taxi ride from the Rampa, or take bus number 84 across from the Vedado Hotel at Humboldt and O Streets)*.

Revolution Square
Obelisk with University
of Havana in foreground

Approaching the square along Rancho Boyeros Avenue, you pass the *Central Bus Terminal*, main travel link between Havana and the rest of the island. Reservations must be made in advance (air-conditioned special service buses cost extra but are well worth it) and tickets must be rechecked at the terminal an hour before departure time. Passengers are allowed 22 kg. plus one piece of hand luggage on these interprovincial buses. In the terminal lobby is an impressive mural depicting the great events and figures in Cuban history.

On your left as you enter Revolution Square is the *National Library*. On your right is the *Ministry of Communications*, where you can purchase stamps, mail letters, send telegrams and check out the history of Cuban communications in the lobby *Postal Museum* — nostalgic penny postcards, postmen's badges, a piece of the first underwater cable laid between America and Europe and the 1939 Cuban postal rocket (a faster-than-airmail experiment that never got off the ground) are among its treasures. Then stop in at the *Postal Shop* for stamp collections, pins, postcards and novelties.

Next to the Ministry of Communications is the *Ministry of the Interior*, with the monumental poster of Che on its facade, and beyond it is the **National Theater**, where local and visiting musicians and dance companies perform.

The statue of *José Martí* and its complementary obelisk form the center of the podium during parades or rallies when Revolution Square is filled with people instead of whizzing cars. Behind the statue are the offices of the *Central Committee of the Communist Party of Cuba*.

Paseo to the Sea

A right turn through Revolution Square leads to Paseo Avenue, a promenade and main thoroughfare lined with schools, hospitals, embassies, private homes and mansions, one of which is the national headquarters of the *Federation of Cuban Women (FMC)*, a must visit for those interested in the advancement of Cuban women.

Two blocks west of Paseo, on 4th Street between Calzada and 5th, the *National Folklore Group* entertains in its leafy patio at *Rumba Saturday*, a rhythmic expression of Afro-Cuban dance and music. Cuban rumba experts of all ages are regularly in attendance and often join in the performance. *Alternate Saturdays at 3 p.m., admission $1 at the gate. Reservations with transportation through hotel tourism bureaus.*

On down 4th Street, at the corner of 3rd, is *Centro Vasco Restaurant*, across a park from the Riviera Hotel. Spanish cuisine and atmosphere at about $15 per person *(tel.: 3-9354 for reservations if you like, but they aren't really necessary).*

Rumba Saturday with the National Folklore Group

Jazz fans should drop in at *Maxim's,* 3rd and 10th Streets, for some of the hottest jam sessions anywhere, featuring Bobby Carcassés' Afrojazz musicians and their improvising guests. *Maxim's is open Monday through Saturday from 2:45 p.m. to 2 a.m. (alternate Saturdays from noon) and Sunday from noon to 2 a.m. Minimum of $3.50.*

Paseo ends at the Malecón, at the flowing *Fountain of Youth,* built in 1978 when the 11th World Youth Festival was held in Havana. The fountain splashes in front of the seaside **Riviera Hotel** ('50s decor and air-conditioned double rooms with private baths ranging from $49 to $62; restaurants, bars, shops, cabaret and a big outdoor swimming pool with poolside bar and cabanas).

A few blocks east of the Riviera, at Malecón and G (Presidentes) Street, the mounted figure of *General Calixto García* guards the shipshape *National Institute of Tourism (INTUR).* Behind INTUR are Cuba's prestigious center of Latin-American arts and letters *Casa de las Américas* and the *Haydée Santamaría Gallery of Latin-American Art.* At the next corner, G and Calzada Streets, the *Presidente Hotel* (four-star elegance with its own topnotch restaurant and an outdoor pool) stands on one corner and the *Ministry of Foreign Affairs (MINREX)* on another.

Miramar

At the western end of the Malecón is the tunnel under the Almendares River that leads to Fifth Avenue, a four-lane boulevard with a center park and promenade that takes you past some of the most luxurious mansions ever built. This is the Miramar neighborhood, still one of Havana's ritziest though most of the great mansions are now embassies, offices, schools, and specialty shops rather than private residences *(buses 32 and 132 will take you from Vedado through Miramar).*

Havana's house of fashion *La Maison* occupies one such mansion at Seventh Avenue and 16th Street in Miramar. Here Cuban designers' clothes are shown in garden fashion shows and sold, along with imported ready-to-wear, accessories and perfumery, in La Maison's shops. Bar, restaurant, sauna and massage services are yours for the asking.

In a white mansion at 6th and 11th Streets in Miramar, *La Flora* sells exclusively Cuban products made in its ten special workshops and by individual artisans: one-of-a-kind dresses from Verano Designers; fine cotton *guayaberas* with the Pepe Antonio label; leather and macramé belts, purses and sandals; copper and brass buckles and wall plaques; wooden figures and boxes; ceramic tableware; marble ashtrays and desk sets; hammocks; and luminous stained-glass lamps and screens that are a modern match for colonial predecessors. Prices at La Flora are considerably under those at La Maison.

Cuba's **National Aquarium** is an extension of the tropical sea it overlooks at 60th Street and 1st Avenue in Miramar. And the Aquarium, unlike the real underwater world, permits you to observe an ominous-looking nurse shark, a mottled moray and a colorful little fairy basslet with equal equanimity. The stars of the Aquarium are *Ciclón* and *Mueve* (Cyclone and Move It), the crooning, dancing dolphins that leap over bars and through hoops, toss balls and race and dive for a delighted kiddy audience every afternoon at 2 p.m. Two of Havana's four-star waterfront hotels are located nearby: the *Tritón* at 70th Street and the *Comodoro* at 84th (double air-conditioned rooms with private baths from $51 to $65).

On the north side of Fifth Avenue, between 110th and 112th Streets is *La Cecilia Restaurant*, one of the best and most charming places to eat in Havana. Carriage gates open into a large courtyard bordered by the lush foliage of a garden restaurant where kitchen and plant aromas mingle in a heady combination. La Cecilia's beef, chicken, fish and pork specialties are cooked Cuban-style and the menu includes a delicious *ajiaco criollo* or Cuban stew, tamales, fried banana chips and a variety of Cuban sweets. Main dishes range from $4 to $9 each. *The restaurant is open daily from noon until the last guest leaves. Phone 22-6700 for reservations or just drop in.*

On the Outskirts

Cuba's **International Conference Center** is an attractive and functional building on a 25-acre plot in the once exclusive residential district of Cubanacán, on the western outskirts of Havana. Its unique architectural design combines modern horizontal lines with a sweeping red-tiled portico typical of the style used in colonial mansions. A fountain plays under the broad entrance stairway leading up to meeting rooms and glass-enclosed corridors overlooking the gardens. Adjacent to the main building is the outdoor-indoor exhibit hall Pabexpo.

Inaugurated for the sixth summit meeting of the Movement of Non-Aligned Countries in 1979, the Center has a plenary hall that seats 2200 delegates, two meeting rooms

International
Conference Center

for 400, one for 150 and seven with capacities of from 60 to 100 as well as the facilities and staff to provide simultaneous interpretation, written translation, multilingual paging, document reproduction, telephone and telex communications, slide projection, closed circuit TV and other technical services. The *Bucán Restaurant,* on the ground floor, serves up to 500 diners in an enclosed, tiled patio with polished wood tables and tropical plants. The Center also has banquet and reception areas; cafeterias; bars; shops; postal, banking and medical services; and parking lots.

Near the Center is a protocol residential area for the delegates and guests who prefer to be closer to the Conference Center than Havana's hotels permit.

Also located in the Cubanacán section is the *National Art School* where the cream of Cuba's young artists, dancers and musicians — selected from all over the island on the basis of their junior high school records — pursue their artistic and academic studies. Visits can be arranged.

Comfort, fishing, privacy and good food are key elements at the **Hemingway Marina**, located 10 miles west of Havana on the coast of the Great Blue River, as US writer Ernest Hemingway called the Gulf of Mexico. Yachts entering the Marina can dock in one of its four canals, each of which has moorings for 100 boats.

Bordering the canals are houses, a shopping center, restaurants and an apartment-hotel with its own pool and cabanas. At the far end of the Marina and connected to it by a narrow causeway is discrete Villa Paraíso, named for a cay Hemingway discovered and returned to again and again. Around the villa's central swimming pool and poolside grill are 25 modern residences separated by spacious gardens. All have private docks and are equipped with everything from dishes to color TV. The Marina will provide cooks, housekeepers, baby sitters and other personnel on request.

The Marina is headquarters for the annual Ernest Hemingway Marlin Fishing Tournament initiated by the US writer in 1950 and several other fishing competitions. It also has a Scuba Club open to foreign residents and visitors. Equipment for all kinds of water sports can be rented at the Marina.

The Marina's three main restaurants are *Papa's* (the lobster is exquisitely prepared), *Fiesta* (name your dish and the chef will cook it to order) and the *Cojímar* in *El Viejo y el Mar* (Old Man and the Sea) *Apartment-Hotel. Tel.: 22-5590/93 for information and reservations. Buses 91, 189, 205 and 218 go to the Hemingway Marina.*

Further west, near the country town of El Chico, is the Ministry of Agriculture's goose farm, a profitable source of goose feathers. Right on the farm is the outdoor ranch-style *La Rueda Restaurant*, named for the big wagon wheel at the entrance and specializing in goose — goose liver, goose steak, roast goose and some 20 other goose dishes. Guests are served the refreshing house cocktail made of rum and fruit juice while they watch a cock fight. The meal starts with a plate of fresh fruit (bananas, watermelon, grapefruit, oranges and mangos), followed by a rich soup. The goose is served with yucca, rice and salad. Accompanying the feast with country music is La Rueda Sextet. *The cost is a flat $20 per person, which can be paid either in dollars or pesos. Telephone 084-25 for reservations and directions.*

To Lenin Park

On the Rancho Boyeros Highway between Havana and José Martí International Airport, you pass *Río Cristal Park,* set back from the road on the banks of the crystal river for which it is named. This refreshing resort has a large swimming pool and two restaurants that serve Cuban dishes at modest prices *(tel.: 44-2396 or 44-1283).*

A turnoff from Rancho Boyeros leads to **Lenin Park**, the 1600-acre playground where Havana's *Pioneer Headquarters* (children's hobby clubs) is located. The park has an amphitheater, an art gallery, a rodeo, riding stables, an open-air movie theater, a tea house, an amusement park, refreshment stands, cafeterias and the stunning *Las Ruinas Restaurant*, built on the ruins of a sugarcane plantation mansion.

Limestone walls covered with moss and ferns are incorporated into the modern marble and stone structure built in

Lenin Park sightseeing train   Boating on Lenin Park lake

Cacti in the Botanical Garden

the late '60s. On the ground floor, three small dining rooms, a bar and a terrace are illuminated by Tiffany lamps and perfumed by the surrounding mastic and pine trees and millenary cycas. From the foyer, a marble staircase leads to the upper floor where a modern stained-glass mural by Cuban painter René Portocarrero glows in the main dining room — furnished with colonial mahogany chairs and tables covered with white linen. Las Ruinas specializes in classic French cuisine featuring Cordon Bleu à Las Ruinas Chicken, Valencian Paella and a variety of beef, pork and lamb dishes. *Average price about $15 per person without drinks. Tel.: 32-4630 for lunch or dinner reservations.*

Outings to Lenin Park with transportation and guide can be booked through the hotel tourism bureau; but if you plan to eat at Las Ruinas, take a taxi (under $10 one way). The bus connections are time-consuming enough to spoil a delicious meal.

The **Botanical Garden** (more than 1000 varieties of Cuban cacti are among its many species) and **National Zoo** (where the animals roam free while the visitors view them from a bus cage) are nearby. Guided tours are the way to see either park. *For advance reservations, call the Botanical Garden at 44-8743 and the Zoo at 44-1870 or 44-2131.*

Where Hemingway Lived

East of Havana, in the little town of San Francisco de Paula, is the Vigía estate, Ernest Hemingway's home from 1939 until shortly before his death in 1961. Now the **Hemingway Museum**, the house contains the writer's furniture, books, trophies and personal effects displayed as they were when he lived there. *The museum is open Tuesday through Saturday from 9 a.m. to noon and 2 to 6 p.m. and Sunday from 9 a.m. to 1 p.m. Tel.: 82-2515.*

In the nearby fishing village of *Cojímar*, the setting for *The Old Man and the Sea*, a bust of the writer stands in the central square. In Cuba, Hemingway is revered as a writer, respected as a fisherman and admired as a rebel. While he wrote and fished, he supported struggles in Spain and Latin America. In 1947, he had to flee Cuba when his contribution to a conspiracy to overthrow the Trujillo dictatorship in the Dominican Republic was discovered. Fidel Castro, then a 21-year-old university leader, managed to escape from Confites Cay on a raft when Cuban troops moved in to quash the anti-Trujillo rebels. Hemingway later aided the 26th of July Movement and publicly declared his support for the triumphant revolution in 1959. He and Fidel Castro finally met at the 1960 Marlin Fishing Tournament.

From Africa to the Arabian Nights

The **Guanabacoa Museum** east of Havana is unique because of its ethnographic rooms containing exhibits on Cuba's African roots and on Afro-Cuban religious practices and symbols. *Open Tuesday through Saturday afternoons and Sunday morning. Tel.: 90-9117. Buses 438, 489 or 493 connect Havana with Guanabacoa.*

Escaleras de Jaruco Park, high in the hills east of Havana, overlooks a vast green valley that stretches across the province to the azure sea. You need a car to get there but it's a wonderful place to spend a restful day. (East on the Thruway to the Tapaste turnoff.) The park has two campsites, picnic areas, cafeterias, a motel and two restaurants.

Perched on the very edge of the topmost peak in the park is a building right out of the *Arabian Nights*: a brick and tile castle with a circular glass-domed tower called *El Arabe Restaurant*. From the tower, a cool bar with cushioned seats in cozy nooks, you step out on the flower-bordered terrace or walk down a flight of stairs to the big main dining room, where the perfumes of Arabia blend under great iron chandeliers and waft over damask-covered tables. On the menu is *Musaka* (chopped beef) for conventional tastes; but lamb is the specialty here and it comes prepared in various ways, all delicious. The supreme treat is certainly *Lashe Mischwuy*, a juicy, tender, perfectly seasoned and cooked lamb en brochette. Prices at El Arabe are modest, the ambience is exotic and the service is impeccable. *Groups should have advance reservations. Tel.: 3-8285.*

Seaside dining at the East Havana beaches

East Havana Beaches

Strung along the north coast to the east of Havana is a jeweled necklace of beaches. A 20-minute car ride brings you to *Bacuranao*, the first beach east of the capital, and an hour's drive will take you out to *Trópico*, the last on Havana's Blue Circuit. In between are *Mégano*, *Santa María del Mar*, *Boca Ciega*, *Guanabo* and *Jibacoa*. All have accommodations (cabanas, houses, villas or hotels) and food (cafeterias, restaurants, snack bars) as well as fine white sand, clear blue water, generally sunny skies and all kinds of recreational facilities. *From the Havana train terminal you can take public bus No. 262 as far as Guanabo and a tourist shuttle service operates between the main beach hotels and the Nacional in Havana. Bus No. 462 from Virgen del Camino, near the Hemingway Museum, also goes to the beaches.*

Santa María del Mar is the longest of these beaches, running roughly from the *José Martí Pioneer City* — where children vacation and study with their classmates and teachers during the school year — to Boca Ciega Beach some 20 miles to the east. Accommodations include *Villa Los Pinos* (27 two- and three-bedroom houses) on the beach, the *Marazul Hotel* (188 air-conditioned rooms with private baths) across from the villa, the 20-room *Atlántico Hotel* on the beach, the new *Itabo* — an Indian word meaning "place of water" — with 198 air-conditioned rooms on a lagoon a few yards back from the beach and five apartment-hotels with a total of 189 rooms.

Each villa and hotel on the Blue Circuit has its own restaurant and also offers a weekly specialty night featuring Cuban food and contagious music. For dining out on your own, try the *Caribe Restaurant-Bar* or the *Guanabo Club*; and the *Pinomar Cabaret* has a good show and dancing.

Days are filled with water skiing, windsurfing, boating, scuba diving, swimming, fishing and such optional excursions as a seafari, a farm party, a Sunday afternoon rumba or a day at *Jibacoa Beach* — a series of shell-shaped inlets with green-robed cliffs rising just behind them — that includes a lobster lunch and, if you like, horseback riding over the hills.

East of this Blue Circuit, *El Abra Campsite* occupies one of the most scenic spots on the Havana-Matanzas shore. The name means open pass and El Abra is on a cove between two coastal peaks whose sharp slopes are pocked with caves framed by tropical vegetation. Just offshore is a coral reef inhabited by brightly colored tropical fish. Used for international tourism during the winter and national tourism during the summer, El Abra has what are probably the best camping facilities in Cuba: 255 pleasant cabanas accommodating from two to six that rent for between $7 and $14 a day, all with private baths and outdoor barbecues. El Abra also has a restaurant-bar, a pool, a rec hall, tennis and volleyball courts, a minimarket that sells canned goods and soft drinks, a first aid post, telephone service and its own buses (for short trips, campers can ride horseback or rent bicycles and mopeds). Snorkeling, scuba diving, underwater photography and windsurfing are among the water sports. All the optional activites at the East Havana beaches are available from El Abra.

East Havana beaches

PINAR DEL RIO PROVINCE

Westward from Havana on the Thruway, the contrasting landscape of Pinar del Río Province emerges. To the north are the craggy heights of the Sierra de los Organos and the Sierra del Rosario mountain chains, whose rivers and streams flow southward toward fields of sugarcane, vegetables and fodder. Scattered throughout the province are small towns and villages, many of them still resistant to the inroads of modern buildings.

SOROA

A 45-minute drive brings you to the turnoff for **Soroa,** a woodsy resort nestled in the foothills of the Sierra del Rosario Mountains.

Soroa's attractions include an orchid garden with hundreds of these plants, a waterfall hidden in the woods, hilly riding trails, an Olympic-size pool, Roman sulphur baths and a selection of snack bars and restaurants. Soroa's charming cabanas are perched along the banks of a gurgling stream and on a hill overlooking the pool.

Horses and bicycles are available at Soroa, but the only way to climb the hills, poke into the caves and reach the waterfall is on foot. Indeed, many who come to the area stay at *La Caridad Campsite* just up the road from Soroa

Soroa

because the hills and woods are more directly accessible from there.

The orchid garden was started by one Tomás Camacho, native of the Canary Islands, who spent nine years building his beloved daughter a hillside house surrounded by a magnificent seven-acre garden of the flowers she most enjoyed. Then, alas, the daughter of the flowers died in childbirth. Her father continued the garden in her memory and added to it rare orchids imported from all over the world. Visitors to this romantic garden, now maintained by the University of Pinar del Río, will find that it contains some 700 species represented in 20,000 plants, of which 250 varieties are indigenous to Cuba.

Deep in the woods near Soroa, a spring-fed stream cascades over a cliff in a small waterfall of postcard perfection. You see it first from above, then follow the path down to the pool below and gaze up through the misty rainbow it forms, feeling rejuvenated, in tune with nature.

Of Soroa's several restaurants, the most special is *El Castillo de las Nubes*, truly a Castle in the Clouds at the top of the highest peak in the area, with a view of the distant Isle of Youth to the south while a miniature Soroa lies at your feet as you gaze northward toward green fields of sugarcane that stretch up to the José Martí Sugarmill on the horizon. The food at El Castillo de las Nubes is as great as the view, featuring crisply fried red snapper or roast stuffed breast of chicken and the seasonal fresh fruit grown in the area — guavas, bananas, oranges, mangos and others. Average price under $10.

Soroa was discovered by Jean Paul Soroa, a French coffee grower who fled the Haitian revolution and arrived in Cuba at the end of the 18th century. There are still families named Soroa in the area and coffee trees planted more than a century ago, some of them on a plantation in the Sierra del Rosario up the road from Soroa. In the early 1970s, a picturesque town named *Las Terrazas* was built there and the terraces were replanted with coffee and other trees as part of a major reforestation program.

MASPOTON

Maspotón, Cuba's main hunting reserve, lies southwest of Soroa in Los Palacios Municipality of Pinar del Río Province. In the rice fields around three big lakes, hunters catch doves, ducks, guinea fowl, pheasants and snipes. Nearby Juventud Reservoir is stocked with largemouth bass while bonefish, snook and tarpon are plentiful off the southern coast at the mouth of the San Diego River.

Maspotón has 14 cabanas, each with two air-conditioned bedrooms and connecting bath, living room-dining room and refrigerator. The club has a restaurant, bar, swimming pool and poolside bar, game room and souvenir shop.

SAN DIEGO DE LOS BAÑOS

Generations of arthritics and rheumatics have visited this spa 120 km. (75 mi.) west of Havana to seek relief from pain. The story goes that a slave, isolated because he had leprosy, happened to bathe in the mineral waters and was cured — which gave the place its fame. In the 19th century, it was widely advertised in the United States as the Saratoga of the Tropics.

LA GÜIRA NATIONAL PARK

This 54,000 acre park-forest, the former estate of Manuel Cortina, lies 40 km. (25 mi.) west of San Diego de los Baños. The estate mansion and its surrounding pagodas are now a museum containing tapestries, statues, porcelain and other furnishings that belonged to the original owner. Surrounding the mansion are a Japanese garden, a formal English garden and a Cuban garden that includes a profusion of butterfly jasmine.

The park's sylvan wilderness makes it a paradise for bird watchers and a confiding deer may appear from time to time. The park's stream, ponds and lakes contain largemouth bass and carp.

Accommodations are in rustic cabins that rise on wooden pillars among the trees. Each has a bedroom, a kitchen, a bathroom and a balcony. The collective showers are at ground level and there's a restaurant nearby.

At the northern end of the park is *Los Portales Cave,* named for the Spaniard who discovered it in 1800. In the late '40s, Cortina used it as his hunting lodge; and, in October 1962, as the world hovered on the brink of the missile crisis, Che Guevara made it staff headquarters for the western army he commanded. It is now one of Pinar del Río's most popular campsites.

PINAR DEL RIO

The provincial capital Pinar del Río is a rambling town whose wooden houses with columned porches give it a turn-of-the-century look. The best accommodations here are at the *Pinar del Río Hotel*: 136 air-conditioned rooms with private baths, a pool, a restaurant, a cafeteria and a rec hall. The hotel is within walking distance, straight down Martí Street, of the *Museum of Natural Sciences* (among its exhibits is the rare cork palm, an indigenous species scientists trace back some 250 million years); the local *History Museum*; the century-old *José Jacinto Milanés Theater*, built of wood with a red tiled roof; *La Casona Restaurant*, which serves Cuban specialties; and the center city shopping area. On the outskirts of the city, in the direction of Viñales Valley, is Pinar del Río's biggest restaurant and cabaret, *Rumayor*. Specialty of the restaurant is the delicious Smoked Chicken Rumayor. The cabaret has a live show and dancing.

Pinar del Río has its own local drink called *La Guayabita del Pinar,* made by adding this small, indigenous fruit and some spices to raw rum and allowing the mixture to ferment. Sometimes a dash of crème de menthe or a shot of aged rum is added before serving. You can order this pleasant, brandy-like liqueur at any bar in Pinar del Río or sample it at the old *House of Garay,* where it was first bottled in 1906.

VINALES VALLEY

Due north of the city are the Sierra de los Organos Mountains, which have extensive caves — some of the largest in Latin America — and wooded slopes that descend into fertile valleys like Viñales, with its marvelous vistas. Here, unique green-robed pincushion bluffs rise from fields where bright green tobacco plants grow. The leaves are picked, sorted, dried and used for cigarettes, pipe tobacco and the renowned Havana cigars — hand-rolled to satisfy discriminating smokers.

The knolls or bluffs in Viñales Valley are pockmarked with caverns, many containing subterranean rivers and falls. One of the best known is the *Indian Cave,* where boats ply the chilly underground waters through capriciously sculptured chambers.

The entire side of one knoll in the valley is covered by an *Archaeological Mural* that traces the evolutionary process in the Sierra de los Organos Mountains, Cuba's oldest outcrop. Painted on the face of the rock are prehistoric ammonites, a marine monster, the huge mammary rodent known as *Megalocnus rodens* and the *Homo sapiens* who first inhabited the region. This monumental mural was executed between 1959 and 1962 under the artistic direction of Leovigildo González, a disciple of the great Mexican muralist Diego Rivera. Some years later, because of considerable damage from rain and sun, the mural had to be

Tobacco field

Archaeological Mural,
Viñales

painstakingly restored by scientists and painters of the National Academy of Sciences, who completed the work in 1980. In the valley below the mural is a pleasant picnic spot with a roofed, open-sided shelter, cooking grills and picnic tables.

For an overview of Viñales Valley, you can drive straight through it to the fishing village of *La Esperanza* on the north shore and set off by boat for a seafood lunch on *Cayo Levisa,* returning to the valley in the late afternoon.

Viñales is also a peaceful Eden for those special vacations that permit an intimate contact with nature. *Los Jazmines Hotel,* with its sweeping view of the entire valley; *Rancho San Vicente,* a spa with mineral waters; and intimate *La Ermita Motel,* just outside the quaint little town of *Viñales,* are the valley's modest lodging houses.

VUELTA ABAJO

The western part of Pinar del Río Province is also known as *Vuelta Abajo,* where net-covered tobacco fields stretch out for miles, interspersed by the gray palm-leaf tobacco houses in which the leaves are dried. The highest quality tobacco, used for export cigars, comes from San Juan y Martínez and San Luis, west of the provincial capital.

On the south coast of the province, 25 km. (15 mi.) west of the provincial capital, is *Bailén Beach*, a mile-long oasis. The resort here has 35 cabanas; a restaurant; two cafeterias; basketball, volleyball and squash courts; and a shooting range.

Continuing west, you reach a chain of lakes — *Cuyaguateje* is the largest — where fishermen regularly catch trophy-size (over 10 pounds) largemouth bass, or *trucha*, as they're called in Cuba. At the western tip of the province is the enormous **Guanahacabibes Peninsula National Park,** a flatland area where the island's main forest, wild life reserves and untapped mineral wealth are located.

THE ISLE OF YOUTH

The Isle of Youth can be reached by hydrofoil or ferry from Batabanó, on the southern coast of Havana Province, or by plane from Havana or Varadero to *Nueva Gerona*.

Foreigners who come for the spectacular scuba diving represent a small fraction of those on the Isle, which is named for the thousands of Cuban and foreign students enrolled in the new boarding schools, who also cultivate

Scuba divers, tropical fish, and coral off the Isle of Youth

Students in Isle of Youth citrus orchards. Ceramics workshop, Isle of Youth

the isle's vast citrus orchards in the work-study program operates throughout Cuba's educational system. The island's annual *Grapefruit Festival* celebrates this important harvest with parades, dancing in the streets and craft exhibits in which local residents, students and touring visitors take part. The foreign students also display their cultural traditions at the *International Festival*, where amateur artists from some 14 African countries, Nicaragua, Korea and Yemen perform.

Next to a children's playground at the entrance to Nueva Gerona is a life-size statue of the milch cow *Ubre Blanca*, who was bred, raised, broke world milk production records and birthed her offspring on the Isle. Sculptors Abelardo Echevarría and Luis Ruz have appropriately immortalized *Ubre Blanca* in the locally quarried marble for which the Isle is so well known.

A HISTORY OF PLUNDER

Other, very different, symbols identified the island between 1494, when Christopher Columbus discovered it on his second voyage to the Americas, and 1959, when dictator Batista was overthrown.

Until well into the 18th century, it was a haven for corsairs and pirates marauding the Caribbean and many ships loaded with gold and precious stones were sunk off the island's coast. No wonder it came to be called Treasure Island, the presumed setting for British writer Robert Louis Stevenson's 19th-century tale of cut-throat villains.

For generations of Cuban revolutionaries, the island was a grim prison. Seventeen-year-old José Martí was held there at **El Abra Farm** — now a museum — before he was exiled to Spain for expressing anti-colonial sentiments in 1870. Fidel Castro and his comrades were confined in the island's so-called **Model Prison** after their conviction for the attack on the Moncada Garrison in 1953. Today, young members of the Pioneers' Organization have their hobby clubs in the former prison and the prison hospital room in which Fidel and his comrades were held is a museum.

Model Prison

When the United States imposed the Platt Amendment on the Cuban Constitution after the Spanish-American War, sovereignty of the Isle of Pines — as it was then called — was left undefined. The US government hoped to sever it from Cuba and annex it to the United States as a kind of island Texas and did succeed in exercising virtual control until 1934, when it was officially declared Cuban territory.

During that period, Americans bought up great tracts of land which they held as absentee owners or, in some cases, developed as cattle ranches or citrus orchards. One of the citrus growers was US poet Hart Crane's maternal grandfather Hart, whose grandson first visited the Isle in 1916 as an impressionable 17-year-old. At his grandfather's orchards near Nueva Gerona, the island capital, young Crane witnessed a devastating hurricane and described the damage in a poem entitled "Eternity:"

The morrow's dawn was dense with carrion hazes
Sliding everywhere. Bodies were rushed into graves
Without ceremony, while hammers pattered in town.
The roads were being cleared, injured brought in
And treated, it seemed. In due time
The President sent down a battleship that baked
Something like two thousand loaves on the way.
Doctors shot ahead from the deck in planes.
The fever was checked. I stood a long time in Mack's talking
Drinking Bacardi and talking U.S.A.

On April 17, 1932, Hart Crane left the Isle of Pines for the United States aboard the *Orizaba*. As the boat moved out of the warm waters he had first known 15 years earlier, Crane went to the rail and, without a word, leaped overboard.

By the late '50s, some 10,000 people lived on the Isle of Pines. Half were prisoners; and the other half were landowners, farmers, fishermen, charcoal makers and a floating population of gamblers, smugglers and prostitutes around the northern freeport of Nueva Gerona. In addition, rich tourists arrived for temporary stays on the other side of the island at the luxurious *Colony Hotel* — which had its own casino and abortion clinic.

TODAY'S WEALTH

Today the four-star Colony is Cuba's *International Scuba-Diving Center*. Accompanied by experienced monitors, divers staying at the hotel board open-deck boats and set off for the island shelf along the so-called Pirates' Coast for a look at some of the most breathtaking underwater landscapes in the Caribbean. There are 17 marked scuba sites with a wealth of coral, sponges, gorgonions, mollusks and tropical fish in the four-mile stretch of sea between Points Francés and Pedernales; and the added enticement of perhaps finding some sunken treasure.

At the eastern tip of the island are the **Punta del Este Caves,** seven coastal caverns containing pre-Colombian Indian pictographs discovered by the survivors of a ship-wreck in 1910. The pictograph in the main cave consists of concentric red and black circles connected by a red arrow pointing east, believed to represent celestial signs used by the Indians. The hotel tourism bureau can arrange visits to the caves.

One of the island's three hunting reserves, mainly for wild boar, is near the caves. Two others, both at Point Francés, have white-crowned pigeons and mourning doves. The *Hunters' Club* adjacent to the Colony Hotel is the island focal point for this sport and hunters often arrive at nearby La Siguanea Airport on charter flights.

On the north coast of the Isle, a half hour's drive from Nueva Gerona, is *Bibijagua Beach,* with its black sand formed by the erosive sea water washing over marble. The beach facilities include a restaurant, a bar, a cafeteria and lockers.

The fine ceramics produced on the Isle of Youth are sold all over Cuba. A visit to the ceramics factory can be arranged through the hotel tourism bureau and pieces can be purchased at the *Juventud Shop* on 39th Street (next to the church) in Nueva Gerona, where you must pay in Cuban pesos, or in the hotel stores, where payment is in foreign currency.

In addition to the luxurious Colony, the Isle of Youth has two three-star hotels much closer to the docks and airport of Nueva Gerona: *Rancho del Tesoro,* just over a mile from town in a woods on the banks of a river (air-conditioned rooms with private baths, radio and telephone from $18 to $27; restaurant, cafeteria, shop and taxi service); and *Las Codornices Motel,* on a lake between the airport and Nueva Gerona (air-conditioned cabanas with private baths, telephone, TV and refrigerators from $18 to $27; restaurant, swimming pool, shop and taxi service).

For eating outside the hotel, try Nueva Gerona's *El Cochinito* for pork and *El Corderito* for lamb, both on 39th Street within a block of each other; or *El Río,* at the corner of 32nd and 33rd, for Cuban specialties. *Average price in all three is around $10.*

CAYO LARGO

Thus it all began! This unspoiled islet at the eastern tip of the Canarreos Archipelago can be reached by plane or boat. A one-day excursion from Havana or Varadero includes round-trip air fare, welcome cocktails and a boat trip to one of the island's seven pristine beaches for a seafood lunch. From Trinidad, on the southern coast of central Cuba, the excursion is by boat.

But most people select Cayo Largo for a longer stay, mainly because it *hasn't* been discovered by the rest of the world. And they aren't disappointed. There's wonderful horseback riding, galloping along miles of sand. Sailing. Windsurfing. Magical fishing expeditions at night. Lazing all alone on an empty, sunswept beach.

The staff on Cayo Largo is especially attentive to their guests' pleasures and whims — in food as well as in recreation. And the accommodations are perfect, too. Charming *Villa Capricho*, on a cliff above the beach, has 50 cabanas with roofs sloping almost to the ground and its own open-air thatched-roof restaurant. Then there's the breezy *Isla del Sur Hotel* which has 143 rooms overlooking a circular swimming pool and the beach beyond. Additional facilities are under construction which, hopefully, will not destroy the ecology and away-from-it-all feeling on this marvelous cay.

Wildlife on Cayo Largo

MATANZAS PROVINCE

VARADERO BEACH

It wasn't until the turn of the century, when the wealthy families of nearby Cárdenas began building summer homes on the north shore of the Hicacos Peninsula, that Varadero became a resort. Before that, because of its inaccessibility, it had been little more than a colonial outpost where small amounts of charcoal and salt were produced. In pre-colonial days, Indians lived on the peninsula and named it for the coco plums that grew along the coast.

With the '20s came land speculation: US industrialist Irénée Du Pont purchased a large beachfront tract and re-

VARADERO

1 Oasis Hotel
2 International Airport
3 Varadero Marina
4 La Cueva del Pirata Cabaret
5 Tourism offices
6 Amphitheater
7 Kawama
8 Punta Blanca
9 La Patana Discotheque
10 Villa Tortuga
11 La Canañita Restaurant
12 Villa Barlovento
13 Mi Casita Restaurant
14 Halong Restaurant
15 Arrecife Restaurant
16 Castel Nuovo Restaurant
17 Villa Sotavento
18 Community Arts Center
19 Bus Terminal
20 Varazul Apartment-Hotel
21 Bellamar Hotel
22 Lai Lai Restaurant
23 Villa Los Cocos

sold part of it as a luxury residential complex. In the '50s, the posh seaside *Internacional Hotel,* complete with gambling casino, went up.

Varadero, a wide beach of sparkling white sand and water shading from turquoise to emerald to indigo, became the Caribbean playground of the rich.

All this began to change in 1959, when 25 new cottages and a beach park with 8000 lockers were built. With the addition of homes, schools, daycare centers and polyclinics, as well as hotels, restaurants and shops, Varadero has now become a very different kind of resort city, with a local population of more than 15,000.

Varadero's top hotels through the '70s were the deluxe *Internacional*, the intimate *Kawama* and the more modest

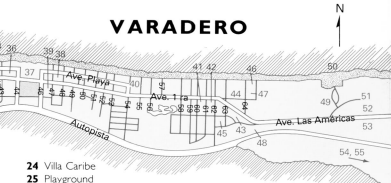

VARADERO

24 Villa Caribe
25 Playground
26 Villa La Herradura
27 Villa Los Delfines
28 El Dastillito Discotheque
29 Post Office
30 Varadero Bookstore
31 El Bodegón Criollo Restaurant
32 Florist
33 Varadero Cinema
34 Library
35 Miniature Golf
36 Pharmacy
37 Coppelia Ice Cream Parlor
38 Pharmacy
39 Fort
40 Albacora Restaurant

41 Villa Cuatro Palmas
42 International Polyclinic
43 Copey Shopping Center
44 International Telephone Center
45 Atabey Hotel
46 Villa Arenas Blancas
47 La Barbacoa Restaurant
48 Siboney Hotel
49 Villa Solymar
50 Internacional Hotel
51 Villa Cabañas del Sol
52 Villa Cuba
53 Meson del Quijote Restaurant
54 Las Américas Restaurant
55 Golf course

Oasis. Then, in 1980, the *Siboney* was constructed across from the beach road on a tract of land that runs right up to Cárdenas Bay. Its sister hotel the *Atabey* was added in 1981 and the *Bellamar*, close to the center of the resort, followed. *Punta Blanca*, at the western tip of the peninsula, is the newest district in the resort with villas and hotels opened in the mid-'80s. All along the beach, big mansions have been remodeled as vacation villas with their own restaurants, bars and recreational facilities. Varadero is still developing, with the construction of 11 new hotels and the remodeling of a dozen villas to be completed by 1990.

Where to Eat

Most villas and hotels feature buffet breakfasts and dinners with plenty of fresh fruit, salads, rolls and pastries baked on the premises and your choice of a main dish. You can walk directly out of the water into any number of seaside restaurants, cafeterias and snack bars or dine out in style, for Varadero has eating places to suit everyone's taste and budget. Moreover, food and service are, for the most part, better than any place else in Cuba.

You won't go wrong if you start with the most famous: *Las Américas,* built as munitions magnate Irénée Du Pont's million dollar winter hideaway — with its own private nine-hole golf course (now open to the public), extensive gardens, white sand beach and landing dock for his yacht and seaplane.

He called the mansion Xanadu. Now, a somewhat tattered banner hanging on the wall in the great main floor dining room quotes Samuel T. Coleridge's poem in elaborately scrolled letters:

> In Xanadu did Kubla Khan
> A stately pleasure dome decree:
> Where Alph, the sacred river, ran
> Through caverns measureless to man
> Down to a sunless sea.´ . . .

The Varadero sea, of course, is sunny; but the allusion to caverns might well apply to the Du Pont wine cellar below the entrance foyer. It was built with five enclaves in the wall, each of which held a barrel of wine. The grilled iron door to the cellar was fitted with a lock whose combination was known only to the master and his wine butler. Du Pont used to entertain business friends at the small mahogany bar next to the wine cellar, where guests now sip drinks and sample delicacies such as oyster cocktails.

On Xanadu's main floor, the foyer opens into an enormous parlor where prospective diners wait to be seated beside an organ that, in Du Pont's days, could be worked hydraulically, electronically and mechanically from the organ room below it. The reverberations were heard a mile away.

In the library, now a second dining room, are leather-bound volumes by some of Du Pont's favorite authors: Balzac, O. Henry, Robert Louis Stevenson and Mark Twain, among others. The library, parlor and dining room face seaward, with floor-to-ceiling windows and doors opening onto the terrace that leads down to the beach.

Off one end of the terrace is the small studio, replica of a schooner captain's cabin, where Du Pont sometimes painted or just gazed out to sea from the porthole.

The mansion's walls, inlaid ceilings and staircases are made of precious Cuban woods: mahogany, ebony and cedar; and the floors are Carrara marble. The nine bedrooms on the second floor all have private bathrooms finished with marble from the Isle of Pines.

The top floor is a roofed ballroom and bar of Italian rococo decor, with a spectacular view of the entire peninsular coast and the Bay of Cárdenas. Deepening tones of transparent blue water reveal a coral reef just offshore. Du Pont held sumptuous private parties here, including the nuptial festivities for his daughters, who were married at sea on the family yacht. The newlyweds then came ashore to spend their honeymoon at Xanadu.

On the beach

Boating from Varadero

People often stop by just to have a look at the mansion. On weekends, especially, Cuban girls celebrating their 15th birthdays appear in the finery of by-gone balls to have their pictures taken in this opulent setting.

Visitors to Varadero who like to dine in elegant surroundings seldom miss the opportunity Las Américas offers: fresh fish or tender beef lovingly prepared and served with decor, efficiency and a pleasant smile. *Located at the end of Las Américas Highway. For reservations, tel.: 6-3415.*

Four smaller restaurants deserve mention for their exquisitely prepared specialties and atmospheric decor: *La Barbacoa*, a tile-roofed country house at the entrance to Villa Arenas Blancas *(64th St. and Ave. Playa, tel.: 6-3435)* grills your T-bone steak or butterfly shrimps to order. *La Cabañita* has a choice of lobster, shrimp, fish filet or filet mignon *(tel.: 6-2215). Mi Casita*, with its charming host and furnishings, offers a choice of lobster, shrimp, fish or filet mignon cooked according to house recipes *(tel.: 6-3787). Halong* serves Vietnamese soups, pork and lobster en brochette and spring rolls against a background of Vietnamese art. The last three are clustered around Villa Barlovento, 11th St. and Camino del Mar. *All four open at 7:30 p.m. and meals run to around $15 per person.*

In the deluxe class is *Universal* in the Internacional Hotel *(tel.: 6-3011),* where crystal chandeliers and stemwear on white damask enhance the splendor of the Châteaubriand steak. *Open from 7 to 10:45 p.m.*

Popular and less expensive are the fish house *Albacora*, with its open dining room and seaside terrace *(59th Street at the beach, tel.: 6-3811); El Bodegón Criollo,* a casual, informal place that specializes in roast pork criollo *(Ave. Playa at 40th St., tel. 6-2180); Castel Nuovo,* for pizzas and Neapolitan ice cream *(tel. 6-2428);* and *Lai Lai,* a Cuban-Chinese restaurant decorated with Oriental vases and screens *(1st Ave. and 18th St., tel. 6-3297). All these restarurants are open for lunch and dinner.*

As for Music

Varadero's cabarets and discos provide hot music and cool drinks and some have shows. Most open at 9 p.m. and close at 3 a.m. The *Continental,* in the Internacional Hotel's former casino, seats over 300 guests for the biggest show in town, dinner, drinks and dancing Tuesday through Sunday. *Tel.: 6-3011 for reservations. La Cueva del Pirata* (Pirates' Cave), as its name suggests, is in a natural cave where the decor speaks to pirate skulduggery. The show is good and so is the dance music. *Open Monday through Saturday at Km. 12 ½ on the Thruway. El Caballito de Coral* is a cozy club in the huge *Varadero Amphitheater,* setting for music and song fests and performances by dance companies. *La Patana* is a floating cabaret in the Paso Malo Canal where guests can drink, dine, dance and enjoy a minishow *(tel.: 6-2849);* and *La Rada* is an attractive disco on the harbor boat dock *(Km. 132 on Vía Blanca, tel.: 6-3108).*In addition, hotels and villas have their own bars and discos with regular or guest musicians.

Most recreation at Varadero, of course, is beach related, with boating, fishing and scuba equipment and excursions available through hotel and villa tourism bureaus and the *Punto Náutico* of the *Bellamar, Internacional, Kawama* or *Oasis Hotels; Villas Barlovento, Caribe* or *Punta Blanca;* the *Marina,* the *Aquarium* and *Punta Francés Campsite.*

International Carnival, in January and February, and the *International Music Festival* are among the festivities held annually at the great blue beach. (See FESTIVALS under SPECIALIZED TOURISM.)

MATANZAS

The provincial capital, 34 km. (22 mi.) west of Varadero, was founded in 1693 and soon became the main port from which pork and beef were shipped to Spain. There are several theories about how it got its name, which means slaughter, the most plausible being that so many animals were sacrificed on its shores.

It was also known as the City of Two Rivers because the *Yumurí* and *San Juan Rivers* flow through it, dividing it into three districts. The fertile soil in the river valleys was planted to tobacco and coffee in the 17th and 18th centuries. But, in the 19th century, Matanzas became the sugarcane capital of Cuba: more than half the island's production came from the plains of Matanzas and its bay was a major slave depot.

Wealthy Matanzans traveled abroad and brought back new ideas that led to the city's cultural development. In the 19th century, Matanzas was nicknamed the Athens of Cuba and was the home of many well-known intellectuals.

The city's three bridges date from that century — before then, precarious wooden bridges connected the three districts or residents used rafts to get about. Matanzas is built around its beautiful bay and up the slopes of a hill that peaks at *Monserrate,* an abandoned shell of a church built in 1873. Below the church grounds to the east, a ferris wheel in a recently opened amusement park turns above the city and the bay. On the other side, the green *Yumurí Valley* stretches westward, cut by the gleaming river and the barely discernible tracks of the electric train that connects Casablanca and Matanzas.

Driving through Matanzas on the Havana-Varadero bayside route, you pass the impressive *Sauto Theater* on La Vigía Square, near the Bailén Bridge over the San Juan River. Built in 1863 at the height of Matanzas' cultural effervescence, the Sauto could always guarantee an elite audience for the stars who performed on its stage: in 1875, the celebrated violinist José White returned to his native

Matanzas for a sell-out concert at the Sauto; Sarah Bern-hardt acted there in 1887; and Ana Pavlova danced there in 1915 — to mention just a few of the greats. During extensive renovation between 1966 and 1969, the gilded ceiling mural representing the nine Muses was restored, wooden floors and iron seats were repaired and new lighting, acoustics and plumbing equipment were installed. Today the Sauto is again on the itinerary of touring musicians, actors and dancers. *Tel.: 2721* for further information. Also on La Vigía Square is the former Junco Palace, now the *Municipal Museum of History. Tel.: 3153.*

Libertad Park, a few blocks inland, has never lost its shady appeal, which is now complemented by restoration of some of the colonial buildings surrounding it. One of these, on Milanés Street, is a century-old mansion-turned-hotel called the *Louvre.* Built around a central patio with a fountain, the hotel is a period piece with polished mahogany furniture, stained-glass windows, majestic crystal chandeliers and antique mirrors in its dining room, bar and lobby. Guests can eat in the elegant dining room or the informal patio restaurant (the menu is the same and the food is excellent at about $5 per person). From the lobby, a great staircase leads to the second floor, where 17 rooms combine modern conveniences with authentic colonial furniture.

In the same block is the former French Pharmacy, now the *Pharmaceutical Museum. Tel.: 3179.* This magnificent apothecary shop was founded in 1882 by Drs. Ernesto Triolet and Juan Fermín Figueroa, lifetime partners in the pharmacy trade, and remained open as a drugstore until 1964. Medications were arranged on the handmade cedar shelves supported by 22 columns along the main wall. The lamps hanging from the hardwood ceilings were imported from Germany. Apothecary's eyes and Sèvres porcelain jars made especially for the pharmacy stand on the long counter. Each month, one of the 55 books of prescriptions filled by the pharmacy between 1882 and 1964 is placed on display.

Also on Milanés Street is Matanzas' oldest church, the *Cathedral of San Carlos*. It dates from 1730 but was extended at later periods in a mixture of styles. The park around the church and the street on which it stands are named for Matanzas poet José Jacinto Milanés.

Ever since its accidental discovery in 1861, *Bellamar Cave*, on Alancía Farm in Matanzas, has been described in speleological superlatives. Its capricious labyrinth of stalagmites and stalactites resembles real waterfalls; enormous crystal chandeliers; heads, profiles and silhouettes of animals; and huge stone fingers. The magical effect of light on walls, ceilings and passageways reveals the memorable Ladies' Salon, the Fountain of the American Maiden, the Tunnel of Love, the Carrot Garden and other wondrous chambers. *Bellamar is open for guided tours from 9 a.m. to 4:30 p.m. every day and a restaurant at the entrance serves typical Cuban food.*

CARDENAS

This provincial city 12 km. (8 mi.) southeast of Varadero is off the beaten track but easily accessible by rented car, taxi or bus if you're staying in Varadero. If you drive to Cárdenas on your own, the very first thing to do is park the car, for this is a city of bicycles and horse-drawn carriages. Everyone seems to use one or the other: bicycles are the individual or family means of travel (many have a child's backseat) for people of both sexes and all ages, while the carriages replace buses and taxis and prove an enchanting way to see the town, moving placidly to the rhythm of hooves.

Cárdenas is a flat city, laid out like a chess board with straight streets, parks and enormous buildings, one of which turns out to be *La Dominica Hotel*, where the Cuban flag was first raised in 1850, when anti-colonialist-annexationist Narciso López unsuccessfully attempted to invade Cuba. Thus Cárdenas is referred to as the Flag City and La Dominica is a national monument. Recently restored, the colonial building has a pleasant moderately priced restaurant at street level and 25 air-conditioned rooms with private baths (doubles cost $10 and singles $8).

Another point of interest is the 19th-century mansion that has been converted into the *José Antonio Echeverría Museum*, birthplace of the university leader and head of the vanguard Revolutionary Student Directorate. On March 13, 1957, Echeverría commanded the takeover of Radio Reloj in coordination with the attack on the Presidential Palace. A few hours later he was shot down on the street. *The museum is located at No. 560 José A. Echeverría. Tel.: 4919.*

The *Oscar María de Rojas Museum* traces the history of Cárdenas and exhibits perfect collections of butterflies and shells. *Tel.: 4112.*

Five kilometers outside the city, at the *Roberto Fernández Farm Cooperative*, in a white-walled, thatched-roof *bohío* that contrasts markedly with the modern housing around it, cooperative members have created Cuba's only *Museum of Peasant Traditions*. Tools, harnesses, pots, water jars and a cart dating from the days of slavery have been collected for the museum, and farmer-guitarists play country music there at evening farm parties or *guateques*.

THE ZAPATA PENINSULA

Located 156 km. (just under 100 mi.) from Havana, 106 km. (65 mi.) from Varadero and 41 km. (25 mi.) from Cienfuegos, the big shoe-shaped (hence its name) peninsula in southern Matanzas Province is a swampy, thickly wooded wildlife reserve and resort area today. In pre-Columbian times it was inhabited mainly by crocodiles and Indians but the conquistadores practically eliminated both. Legend has it that the invaders were unable to seize the Taíno Indians' treasure, for the natives threw it into the lake — which has since been known as Treasure Lake — rather than surrender it. After the Spaniards continued inland to occupy more fertile farm land, the peninsula was largely abandoned. At the triumph of the revolution in 1959, a handful of charcoal makers and fishermen eked out a poor living there. Then the Zapata began to change as roads, schools, houses, polyclinics and a picturesque resort were built.

Guamá, named for a brave Indian chief who fought the Spanish invaders, was the first resort built by the new government. It is a reconstructed Taíno Indian village with thatched-roof cabanas rising on pillars over *Treasure Lake*. Bridges connect the rustic-looking but comfortably appointed cabanas with the shore where the restaurant, cafeteria, pool and boutique are located. Indian artifacts are the treasures that have been found on the Zapata Peninsula and in Treasure Lake itself and some are exhibited in the *Guamá Museum*.

On one of the islets in Treasure Lake is an Indian village inhabited by 25 life-size figures of Indians engaged in daily activities, the work of Cuban sculptor Rita Longo.

Treasure Lake is noted for the size and abundance of its largemouth or black bass (*Micropterus salmoides*) and is also home to tortoises, bullfrogs, tarpon and the curious *manjuarí*, a meter-long cross between a fish and a reptile that inhabited the earth in primitive times.

At the entrance to the resort is the crocodile breeding farm that ensures the survival of these ancestral inhabitants and onetime rulers of the peninsula. Next to it is the excellent *Boca de la Laguna Restaurant* and the *Ceramics Workshop* that produces the pottery used in the Boca, in airy *Pío Cuá Restaurant* at the entrance to the Zapata and at the beach

Heading for Guama

Birders on the Zapata Peninsula

Playa Larga

villas. The attractive, chunky pieces are also sold at the workshop.

The Zapata Peninsula is considered Cuba's major wildlife reserve, where the fauna are protected and a constant watch is kept on environmental features. Along its trails, bird watchers have spotted such rare and endemic species as the tiny bee hummingbird; the Zapata sparrow; the yellow-shafted flicker; Gundlach's hawk; the red, white and blue national bird, the Cuban trogan; and many others.

The Peninsula also has two fine beach resorts: **Playa Girón** (Bay of Pigs) and **Playa Larga**, both with tourist accommodations and the former with a museum that documents the mercenary invasion defeated there in April 1961.

VILLA CLARA PROVINCE

East of Matanzas, the province of Villa Clara runs from the Atlantic Ocean on the north coast to the Escambray Mountains in the south, with Cienfuegos on the southwest and Sancti Spíritus on the east. Santa Clara, the provincial capital, is a hub with spokes leading to all parts of Villa Clara.

SANTA CLARA

If you're staying in this city of contrasts, your first stop may well be *Los Caneyes*, a motel that resembles a pre-Columbian Indian village of circular wooden huts or *caneyes*, with conical thatched roofs like those the Siboney and Taíno Indians built. Although these *caneyes* have all the conveniences the Indians lacked, their rustic appearance and wooded setting make them seem very distant from 20th century urban life.

Yet just down the road from this idyllic setting are the structures that most clearly represent a rapidly developing city: the big INPUD factory inaugurated by Che Guevara in 1964, which produces refrigerators, stoves, pressure cookers, expresso coffee makers and other housewares for domestic sale; numerous agroindustrial plants and warehouses; hospitals and polyclinics; apartment buildings, neighborhood schools, stores and offices. In the other direction is the educational strip bordered by the May 1st Boarding School for high school students; the Manuel Ascunce Domenech Teachers' Training School, named for the young teacher who was killed by counterrevolutionaries during the Literacy Campaign of 1961; and the enormous campus of the Central University.

Where the main railway line enters the city, four boxcars and a bulldozer next to the tracks form the *Armored Train Monument*. The exhibits inside the cars show how guerrillas under Che Guevara's command derailed a train loaded with enemy troops and US Army weapons in the decisive battle of Santa Clara preceding the triumph of the revolution on January 1, 1959.

Further evidence of that battle is preserved in the shrapnel-pocked facade of the *Santa Clara Libre Hotel* on Santa Clara's main square, surrounding *Leoncio Vidal Park*.

Named for a hero of Cuba's War of Independence against Spain, the park provides continuity between that colonial era and present-day Santa Clara. Its graceful gazebo is still used for municipal band concerts; its leafy *guásima* and poinciana trees continue to provide night shelter for Cuban blackbirds and sparrows, who warble like alarm clocks at dawn; and its double sidewalks — formerly separated by an iron fence that demarked the inner strolling space for whites from the outer area for blacks — are now a meeting place for students on their way to classes, workers on their lunch break and oldsters sunning on park benches.

At one corner of the square is the *Caridad Theater*, erected by Marta Abreu de Estevez in 1884-85 in memory of her parents "for the poor of Santa Clara."

The wealthy Abreu family was also responsible for Santa Clara's first free clinic, still operating as part of the national network of health facilities, and a free primary school. Located a block away from the main square, the primary school was established in 1878 by Don Pedro Abreu and supported by his daughters after his death. Later it became a convent and then a trade school. After the triumph of the revolution, it was headquarters for the Santa Clara Ministry of Education for several years until the impetuous expansion of Cuba's educational system forced the Ministry into larger, more modern offices.

Then the lovely colonial building was completely restored and reopened in 1966 as the **1878 Restaurant,** a perfect place to wind up a tour of Santa Clara.

REMEDIOS

Remedios, with a population of 16,500, is a city with a 400-year-old history and an annual fiesta whose origins go back more than 250 years. Founded in 1524 on a cay off the north coast of what is now Villa Clara Province in central Cuba, the settlement was besieged by pirates, who forced the people to move twice. To escape further attacks and rid themselves of the "infernal legions of demons" prophesied by their priests, 18 Remedian families fled inland and founded the city of Santa Clara in 1689. Then, in a misguided effort to persuade the remaining Remedians to join them, some returned and sacked their hometown, destroying everything except the church.

By the 18th century, however, Remedios was an established villa with two churches, two schools and an active social life. The rustic 16th-century church was greatly expanded and the feast of San Juan, originally a purely religious celebration in honor of Remedios' patron saint, spilled into the streets in a people's fair of costumed parades, music and typical food.

Around the Square

In the early 19th century, Remedios was practically destroyed by fire and most of the existing colonial buildings were erected after that. Arms Square — now *Martí Park* — was constructed between the old *San Juan Bautista Church* and the newer *Buen Viaje Church* in 1852. The mansions and public buildings around the square also date from that period.

On the north side is the graceful family home of Alejandro García Caturla, the brilliant composer who broke with all bourgeois conventions. Born into a wealthy Remedian family of artists and patriots, Caturla identified with the Afro-Cuban roots, rituals and sufferings of the poor, reflecting them in his art, his marriages to black women and his incorruptibility as a lawyer and judge — for which he was assassinated in 1940 at the age of 34. Now the *Alejandro García Caturla Music Museum*, the mansion has been renovated and was reopened in 1987, on March 7, the date of his birth in 1906. It contains his manuscripts, musical instruments — except the saxhorn he played in *Las Parrandas*,

Remedios

which is displayed in the nearby museum devoted to that traditional fiesta — biographical material, personal effects and tapes of his modern, avant-garde music as well as material on other Remedian musicians. A few steps away, a mansion built in 1875 is now the attractive *Colonial Restaurant*.

Across the square from the Music Museum is the historic *Mascotte Hotel* where Liberation Army General Máximo Gómez met with President McKinley's personal envoy Robert Proctor on February 10, 1899, to negotiate the terms of the Mambí fighters' honorable discharge following the Spanish-American War. Gómez occupied the spacious corner suite overlooking the square during the two days he stayed at the Mascotte.

Recently remodeled, the hotel now has private baths adjoining each of its 14 air-conditioned rooms with their colonial-style furnishings (the suite the General used has a canopied four-poster bed). In the flower-tiled lobby, a marble-topped table and straight chair like those Gómez used are roped off below a wall plaque commemorating the historic meeting. The wood-paneled dining room and bar adjacent to the lobby open through arched doorways onto a flagstoned patio with a center well.

Running along the east side of the Square is the *San Juan Bautista Church*, its plain limestone facade belieing the rococo splendor within. Badly damaged by an earthquake in 1939, the church was restored over a ten-year period (1944-1955) by a millionaire penitent. Most of the interior is the work of Cuban artist Rogelio Atá, who did the main altar in elaborately carved cedar encrusted in 24-carat gold leaf. Great arches separate the side aisles from the center nave whose vaulted Moorish ceiling is carved mahogany painted with black scrolls and, near the altar, gold relief. San Juan Bautista Church is a fabulous religious museum in this colonial city declared a national monument in 1979.

Other historic buildings on Martí Square are the *Young Peoples' Social Center*, known as the Tertulia in 1895 when most of its members went off to fight for Cuba's independ-

ence; and the *Remedios Workers' Club,* in the former Casino
Español where Máximo Gómez was feted at a postwar banquet to heal the breach between opposing sides in Cuba's
War of Independence. Commercial establishments — a
market, a cafeteria, several shops and two newsstands —
also line this busy central square.

The *Remedios History Museum* — where any tour of the
city should begin — the *Public Library* (successor to the first
library in the interior of the island, established in Remedios
in 1864), the fascinating *Las Parrandas Museum* and the *Community Arts Center* are all nearby in the old city, with its red-
tiled roofs and narrow streets where horse-drawn carts,
bicycles and feet are still the main means of transportation.

Las Parrandas

No description of Remedios would be complete without a
word about its passionate *Parrandas.* The whole town turns
out for this one-night contest of towers, lanterns, banners,
floats and fireworks presented by the neighborhoods of
Carmen — whose symbol is the sparrowhawk and a globe
— and San Salvador — identified by a rooster. Months of
preparation precede it.

The form and artistic elements of *Las Parrandas* were set
in the late 19th century. The traditional polkas played to
announce alternating neighborhood presentations were
composed by local musicians in 1880, making Remedios the
only Cuban city where the eminently Polish polka is as indigenous as the spontaneous rumbas of challenge and victory that also accompany *Las Parrandas.*

Alternately throughout the night, Carmen and San Salvador present their artisan collections of glowing lanterns,
insignias, banners and pyrotechnics that fill the square
with flashes of light, deafening explosions and smoke so
thick you can't see across Martí Park. Just before dawn, the
two neighborhood floats move slowly around the square
and halt facing each other. There, on glittering stages, the
respective themes are echoed in strikingly costumed tab-
leaus.

Then both sides parade into the opposing neighborhood and joyfully proclaim victory — which is as it should be in Remedios where the people are *parranderos* from cradle to grave. This memorable celebration takes place on the last free (non-working) Saturday before year's end.

CAIBARIEN AND CAYO CONUCO

From Caibarién, a fishing village on the coast a few kilometers northeast of Remedios, the offshore cays seem to be an extension of terra firma separated from it by placid lakes. In fact, the first settlement in these parts in the early 16th century was established on the closest of these islets, Cayo Conuco.

Now a 15-minute motorboat ride takes you from the port of Caibarién to Conuco's wooden dock, where a sign welcomes you to the 363-acre cay. From the dock, a trail leads up the hill to what must be one of Cuba's most inviting campsites: rustic cabanas hidden in the woods overlooking the water — where campers are always swimming and fishing — a store; movie, TV and dance areas; a rec hall; a campfire circle; a stable where 20 horses await riders; outdoor cooking areas; guaranteed cold drinking water, ice and fresh bread brought daily from the mainland; group shower and toilet facilities; and then the things that are special to the cay such as sea treasure hunts and nature walks (Cayo Conuco has 172 plant species and 72 harmless animals including iguanas and hutías).

Nearly 20,000 campers and one-day excursionists use the cay's camping facilities annually. The one-day outing includes lunch at a charming hillside restaurant, which also serves the cay's little six-room hotel. Both these facilities next to the campsite are run by the Caibarién Food Industry and are open to campers, too.

In Caibarién itself accommodations are available at the seaside *Brisas del Mar Hotel* (15 rooms) and the portside *España Hotel* (11 rooms), which also serves the best seafood in town. By prior arrangement with the Villa Clara Tourism

Enterprise, groups from abroad are accommodated at the luxurious seaside *Military Hotel* and their options include day trips to the more distant Cayo Fragosa, with swimming, fishing and a beach picnic.

ELGUEA BATHS

Also in northern Villa Clara Province, near Corralillo, are the Elguea Baths, a health spa centered around medicinal waters that relieve rheumatic, neurological and circulatory problems as well as minor skin irritations and respiratory distress. Guests walk or take the tractor-pulled bus from the modern hotel (106 double rooms with private baths) and cabanas (33 beds) to the thermal pools, carbonic foot bath, sulphuric mud and refreshing shampoo baths. The hotel also has a pool and a physiotherapy room. A medical staff specialist, three nurses, a physiotherapist and a physical education director are on hand to advise guests and supervise therapy programs. Many of the Cubans you meet at Elguea are repeaters who swear by the curative effects of the baths. Sometimes a doctor recommends Elguea but most people make their first visit on the basis of word-of-mouth experiences at the baths.

LAKE HANABANILLA

The Sierra del Escambray, one of Cuba's three great mountain ranges, rises splendidly to the south of Santa Clara. From the provincial capital, the road winds past fields of sugarcane and small towns with a single main street to *Manicaragua*, where a right turn leads to the *Hanabanilla Hotel* overlooking the lake.

Although the hotel is on a hilltop, it nestles into the breathtaking scenery without overriding it: simple, sober, a proper place for rest and tranquility. The surrounding mountains reaffirm that image.

Below the hotel is the dock, at the edge of the artificial lake that extends throughout what was once a valley — it's

Lake Hanabanilla from Rio Negro Restaurant

so big you can barely make out the houses on the opposite shore. Next to the hotel, at the top of what used to be a waterfall, is the modern hydroelectric plant that supplies power to the entire region.

There are rowboats for the fishermen who can't wait to catch largemouth bass and launch trips across the lake to *Río Negro Restaurant,* with its palm-thatched huts perched on a hillside at the top of a steep path bordered by bougainvillea vines, coffee plants and ancient trees. From here, the lake is an amethyst framed by emerald foliage. Then, as you approach the restaurant, even the marvelous scenery is overshadowed by the tantalizing aroma of roast pork wafting over rustic tables and wooden chairs with goatskin seats.

Stopping at one of the small farms on the shore of Lake Hanabanilla, you may see piles of beans from which the rich local coffee is made, buzzing bee hives and the golden honey they produce, farm animals — horses, dogs, chickens, pigs and iridescent peacocks — and the typical *bohío* farm house, always equipped with electric refrigerator and TV.

The Hanabanilla Hotel has 128 air-conditioned double rooms with private baths, a restaurant and bar, a swimming pool with poolside bar and grill, a roof terrace-bar, a game room and shops.

CIENFUEGOS PROVINCE

Cienfuegos, on the south-central coast of Cuba, is a 335-km. (nearly 210-mi.) drive east from Havana on the Thruway and its Cienfuegos spur. Daily trains with Fiat air-conditioned coaches, reserved seats and snack service leave Havana's Tulipán Station (one-way fare five pesos), but that trip takes about eight hours because of the number of stops.

When you speak of Cienfuegos, however, you have to begin with its bay, whose life and luminosity reign over the city known as the pearl of the south. A narrow, winding channel leads into this shell-shaped body of water dotted with cays and islets that Louis de Clouet, a French planter from Louisiana, saw was key to the prosperity of the settlement he and 45 colonists from Bordeaux founded there in 1819 with the approval of Cuban Governor José Cienfuegos.

The pretty seaside city prospered on the basis of the sugarcane, tobacco and fruit grown in the fertile farmlands around it and so easily loaded for shipment from the bay.

Perché fishing village in Cienfuegos Bay

Today motorboats, fishing boats, sightseeing yachts and the appealing *pesetero* ferries streak the bay and cargo ships load and unload at its wharfs. The bay shore is a picturesque landscape of houses and lush foliage, with the bulk sugar loading terminal, fertilizer factory and Cuba's first nuclear power plant (still under construction) on the western shore and the *Jagua* and *Pasacaballos Hotels* and the sentinel fortress *Jagua Castle* rising to the east.

Built in 1745, Jagua Castle is the city's oldest structure. It was designed to stop the smuggling that flourished between townspeople and pirates and protect the canal leading into the bay in case of a pirate attack. According to legend, the Jagua is haunted by a Blue Lady who appears during the night to protect the area.

Below the fort and protected by it is the picturesque fishing village of *Perché*, where most of the houses are built on piles at the water's edge. Some are wooden castles, others simple dwellings; but almost all have red tile roofs and multiple doors and windows to admit the sea breeze.

In the Punta Gorda district, the Jagua Hotel, a luxury gambling resort before 1959, has excellent accommodations with a view of the bay. Next to it is the exotic Gothic-Moorish-Venetian *Valle Palace*, now a restaurant and souvenir shop. Ferries cross the channel to the Pasacaballos Hotel, which dominates a hill 15 miles outside Cienfuegos by road.

Downtown

Cienfuegos' main artery, the Prado Promenade, is a long central park bordered with trees and benches that runs out to the Punta Gorda peninsula and downtown to *Martí Park*, where the French settlers first broke ground. Traffic flows along both sides of this promenade, past stores, restaurants, schools, theaters, ice cream parlors and houses.

An airy gazebo stands at the center of Martí Park and Square, which has been declared a national monument. All the buildings around the square were built in the 19th or early 20th century and are significant landmarks in the city's history: the handsome stone *Cathedral,* blessed as a church in 1867 and raised to the level of Cathedral in 1904, with masterful stained-glass windows depicting the Twelve Apostles; the handsomely wood-paneled, frescoed, three-tier *Tomás Terry Theater,* named for a millionaire sugar planter and inaugurated by his heirs in 1890; the *Primer Palacio,* now the seat of *Peoples' Power;* the *Museum of History;* and the *San Lorenzo School.*

When sailors at the Cienfuegos Naval Base rose up against the Batista regime on September 5, 1957, students at the San Lorenzo School joined the rebellion and, together, they held the city for several hours. The *National Naval Museum,* on 21st Street between 60th and 62nd, commemorates that action and recently built socio-cultural installations have been named for it.

Cienfuegos' restaurants reflect the city's varied culinary tradition: *Covadonga* for paellas; *1819* for Cuban fare; *El Polinesio* for international cuisine; *El Cochinito* for pork; and *La Laguna* for seafood.

On the Outskirts

Twenty-three kilometers (15 mi.) west of Cienfuegos — a stop on the Havana-Cienfuegos train — is the *Ciego Montero Spring,* a medicinal-mineral spa with a hotel, pool and individual baths. Most of the carbonated mineral water served in Cuban restaurants is bottled in Ciego Montero, which is pictured on the label.

Sixteen kilometers (10 mi.) east of Cienfuegos, on the road to Trinidad, is the *Botanical Garden* started by Harvard University around 1910. Some 2000 species grow there now, including more than 200 varieties of cacti, 300 palms and all 23 types of butterfly jasmine, Cuba's national flower.

Nearby is the road to *Rancho Luna Beach,* a popular resort with a modern 225-room hotel (air-conditioned rooms with private baths) and facilities for every type of beach activity. Like the Jagua and Pasacaballos, the Rancho Luna Hotel offers sightseeing in and around Cienfuegos and excursions to other parts of the island.

SANCTI SPIRITUS PROVINCE

TRINIDAD

The city of Trinidad, in Sancti Spíritus Province, nestles into the foothills of the Escambray Mountains overlooking the Caribbean coast, just off the highway that connects Cienfuegos and the provincial capital Sancti Spíritus. A more adventurous way to reach Trinidad is to take the winding road across the Escambray from Manicaragua to *Topes de Collantes*. Built as a tuberculosis sanitarium in the '50s, Topes de Collantes became a teachers' training school in the '60s, after tuberculosis had been eradicated, and is now used for health tourism (See SPECIALIZED TOURISM). From there the road continues in hair-pin turns down to Ancón Beach and Trinidad.

Sugar and Slavery
One of Cuba's oldest villas, Trinidad is the most perfectly preserved colonial city on the island. Its cobblestoned streets, red tile roofs, balustered windows and stained-glass arches take you back to another era.

Colonial Trinidad   Trinidad street   Weaver

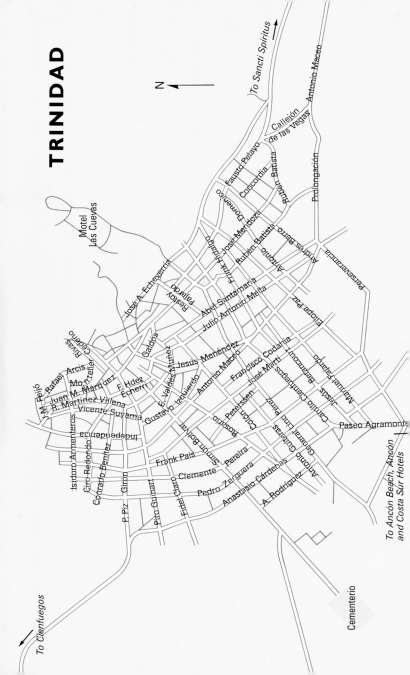

Trinidad's *Main Square* was a small Indian settlement when Diego Velázquez founded the villa in 1514. Five years later, Hernando Cortés set up camp there while he obtained provisions, horses and men for the conquest of Mexico. During the 16th and 17th centuries, Trinitarians raised cattle, sugarcane and tobacco. To circumvent trade restrictions imposed by the Spanish Crown, they were up to their necks in contraband — known as the salvage trade.

Trinidad's boom period occurred after the Haitian Revolution and before the Cuban War of Independence — roughly from 1817 to 1862 — when sugar and slavery were the sources of the villa's wealth. Slaves worked the plantations and mills owned by whites, many of whose fine homes were designed and built by free black artisans. In 1827, Trinidad had more tiled-roof and mortar houses in proportion to its population than any other city on the island.

By that time, Trinidad's Main Square looked very much like it does today: royal palms, bougainvillea and roses growing in a central park enclosed by a wrought-iron fence; and around the cobblestoned square, the *Santísima Trinidad Church* and the residences of the most exalted members of colonial Trinitarian society: the house of Alderman Ortiz (*Guamuhaya Archaeological Museum*), the Padrón house (*Alexander von Humboldt Museum of Natural Sciences*), Count Brunet's Palace (*Romantic Museum*), and the Sánchez Iznaga house (*Museum of Trinitarian Architecture*). The Brunet Palace was built by slave traders who displayed their wealth in marble floors, mahogany stairways and the kind of luxurious furnishings now exhibited in the Romantic Museum.

Until just a few years ago, descendants of the Sánchez Iznaga family lived in what has since become the Museum of Trinitarian Architecture, composed of two single-story houses built side by side, one in the 18th and the other in the 19th century. These two houses and the exhibits of structural sections rescued from other Trinitarian buildings reveal architectural innovations, fine craftsmanship and an opulent lifestyle. The museums's high-ceiling rooms open onto a patio enclosed by service and storage rooms on either side and a back wall covered with jasmine. The great mango tree in the garden still bears luscious fruit in season and shades flower beds and pots filled with malanga, begonia, ferns and other exotica.

Near the Main Square is the former San Francisco de Asís Convent, now the *Museum of the Struggle against Bandits,* referring to the counterrevolutionary bands weeded out of the nearby Escambray Mountains in the early sixties. From its bell tower, you see Trinidad's tile-roofed houses, the tower of Trinidad's oldest church *Nuestra Señora de la Candelaria de la Popa,* children playing in the streets, the blue sea and distant Potrerillo Peak in the Escambray.

In *Real del Jigüe Square,* where one of the house fronts is ingeniously and decoratively hand-painted (facade and wall murals are characteristic of Trinidad), a plaque honors Father Bartolomé de las Casas, defender of the Indians, and a calabash tree commemorates the first mass, held by Franciscan Father Juan de Tesín in 1514.

Trinitarian Traditions

The place to stop for refreshments in Trinidad is *La Canchánchara,* named for the local drink served there, which is made with lime juice, honey, aguardiente (raw rum) and ice. Except for the ice, it's the drink the Mambí liberation fighters downed before going into battle against the Spanish troops. For a full meal, the *Colonial Trinidad Restaurant (55 Maceo Street, tel.: 2873)* provides the appropriate setting for excellent food and the nearby *Guamuhaya* is on a par. *Prices at both run from about $3.60 to $6.60 à la carte.*

Continuing through the cobblestoned streets of Trinidad, the visitor can observe old iron street lamps; arched windows; grillwork; wooden portals, balustrades and roofs; wall friezes painted in every color; a glimpse of antique furniture through an open window; and Trinitarians moving with their provincial, Caribbean rhythm: the woman seated placidly on the sidewalk knitting baby booties, another weaving straw hats as she chats, the farmer in his mule-drawn cart, the milkman with his cans on horseback, the bird-cage maker and the potter turning the wheel with his foot.

One of the narrow streets leads to *La Casa de la Trova* or Troubadours' House — where music, dancing and drinking continue far into the night.

Accommodations in Trinidad are available in the pleasant cabanas of *Las Cuevas Motel*, on a hill overlooking the city; or at *Ancón Beach,* where the modern *Costa Sur Hotel* has 70 air-conditioned rooms with private baths, and the spanking new *Ancón Hotel* has 209 air-conditioned rooms with private baths. Off Ancón Beach are 17 marked scuba sites.

Sugarmill Valley

Between Trinidad and Sancti Spíritus lies the **San Luis Valley,** also known as Sugarmill Valley because some 43 sugarmills operated there in the mid-19th century at the height of Trinidad's sugar production. The most striking structure in this valley is the 45-m.- (150-ft.) high *Manacas-Iznagas Tower*, built by the wealthiest Trinitarian sugar baron of the 19th century. Other landmarks include plantation mansions, slave quarters and slave cemeteries. Indeed, the entire valley is Trinidad's fascinating Museum of Slavery.

Manacas-Iznagas tower

SANCTI SPIRITUS

One of the first seven villas, Sancti Spíritus was founded in 1514 on the banks of the Tuinicú River, but the settlers were soon driven to the present site on the Yayabo River to escape a plague of biting ants.

Pirates attacked the villa on numerous occasions, destroying the *Parroquial Mayor Church* built in 1522 in one of their raids. Between 1671 and 1680, the church was rebuilt using the original bricks and stones. The tower was added in the 18th century and the cupola in the 19th. The church stands at the center of the historical section of the city and all the buildings around it also date from the colonial period. Of special pride to city residents are the charming houses on *El Llano Street,* which communicates with another point of historical interest, the *Yayabo River bridge,* built in 1825 and now the only arched stone bridge that remains in Cuba.

Sancti Spíritus, located on the Central Highway, is also the center of the province's agroindustrial development for it is surrounded by fields of sugarcane that feed the *Uruguay Sugarmill,* largest in the country, and provide the bagasse used in the modern Jatibonico paper mill. Because Sancti Spíritus was never completely bypassed as Trinidad was, its historical landmarks are surrounded by modern buildings and the busy city lacks the timeless, museum-like perfection of Trinidad.

Just outside the city is *Lake Zaza,* a big artificial lake famous for its largemouth bass. In the woods around the lake, hunters find mourning and white-winged doves. The modern *Zaza Hotel* on the banks of the lake accommodates fishermen, hunters and others in 128 air-conditioned rooms with private baths. The hotel also has a restaurant, bars, swimming pool and game room and rents fishing and hunting gear. Nearby is *Los Laureles Motel,* with 104 cabanas, two restaurants and three bars.

CIEGO DE AVILA PROVINCE

A flat province stretching across the island between Sancti Spíritus and Camagüey, Ciego de Avila has vast sugarcane plantations and extensive truck farms and orchards: pineapple, bananas and all the citrus fruits are grown in this province. The main highway passes through the city of *Ciego de Avila,* provincial capital, which has a comfortable hotel of the same name on its outskirts. For most visitors, though, there's no tarrying in this part of the province and they turn north for hunting and fishing in the coastal low-lands and lakes or a trip to an offshore cay.

MORON

Morón, in the northern part of the province, is the ideal base for these activities. The *Morón Hotel* has 144 air-conditioned rooms with private baths, telephone and radio; a good restaurant; several bars; swimming pool; tennis court; shops; beauty parlor; barbershop; game room. A block from the hotel, you can hire a horse-drawn carriage for a pleasant drive around town.

The bronze rooster perched at the entrance to the hotel's sweeping driveway is the symbol of Morón and its people: a fighting cock that crows loudly every day at 6 a.m. and 6 p.m.

Just outside the city is the *Morón Reserve,* where hunters bag mourning doves and white-crowned pigeons. To the north of the city is *La Leche Lagoon,* so named because of its

Morón's buggy terminal

milky-colored water due to sodium carbonate deposits. Snooks and tarpons inhabit the lake, which is often used for sailboat regattas. East of it is the smaller *La Redonda Lake,* where bass fishermen rendezvous.

The *Aguachales de Falla Hunting Club,* in the swampy area near the coast, is a reserve of woods surrounding small- and medium-sized lakes and ponds linked by canals. Mallards and fulvous tree ducks are the favorite prey at Aguachales.

The highway north of these lakes runs to *Turiguanó Isle,* a 44,460-acre cattle ranch where herds of ruddy St. Gertrudes are raised. The little town at its center, established in 1959, has houses built with the slanted roofs and chimneys of a colder clime.

A 17-km. (11-mi.) causeway from the north coast of Morón Municipality out to Cayo Coco now provides easy access to that 360 sq. km. (140 sq. mi.) island with its 30 km. (20 mi.) of fine white beaches. The cay is presently inhabited by wild horses, cattle and pigs; a great variety of birds, including rare and rosy flamingos; and a handful of people. While remaining a wildlife sanctuary, the cay will become the province's main beach, with an infrastructure of roads, electricity, water and sanitation. Later, lodgings and an airport will be built.

CAYO GUILLERMO

The boat for Cayo Guillermo leaves from the docks of the Punta Alegre fishing cooperative, 67 km. (44 mi.) northwest of Morón. After plying through the blue-green sea on the island shelf, the boat enters a channel with cays and little islets on either side — all part of the archipelagos that extend along the north coast of Cuba from Cárdenas Bay, in Matanzas, to Nuevitas Bay, in Camagüey. Cayo Guillermo — just over 12 sq. km.(5 sq. mi.) in area — lies 23 km. (15 mi.) offshore on the seaward side of Cayo Coco.

The cay's three sandy beaches are protected by a coral reef that scuba divers explore with endless fascination.

Fishermen hook bonefish, flounder, groupers, jacks, mackerel, snappers and snooks around the cay. Further out, toward the Great Bahama Bank, the coveted beaked fish run from April through June.

On Cayo Guillermo, *Villa El Paso* or *la casita* as everyone calls it, has eight double air-conditioned rooms with private baths, restaurant and bar. Anchored just off the cay is the *Last Paradise* floating hotel, the only one of its kind in Cuba. Built on a sugar barge at the Baraguá and Júcaro docks in southern Ciego de Avila Province, this steel and wood *patana* or flat-bottomed boat was originally launched in *Los Jardines de la Reina Archipelago* off the southern coast of Ciego de Avila Province, where it remained from 1981 to 1985. Then an experienced crew took it half way around the Cuban coast to the more accessible north shore cay, leaving Los Jardines de la Reina in September 1985, stopping at La Alameda docks in Santiago de Cuba for a month and a half and reaching Cayo Guillermo on December 20. The double-decked hotel has 12 air-conditioned rooms with private baths on the upper deck and a restaurant-bar, lobby, boutique and poop deck below. Those who have stayed at the Last Paradise say it lives up to its name.

CAMAGUEY PROVINCE

Largest in area and sixth in population, Camagüey Province is cattle raising country where cowboys on horseback driving their herds from one pasture to another can stop traffic on any country road. Even so, billowing fields of sugarcane occupy more acreage than grazing lands.

CAMAGUEY

The provincial capital was founded in 1514 as *Santa María del Puerto Príncipe* near what is now the busy industrial port city of *Nuevitas*, then transferred to the banks of the Caonao River where the soil was better and there was fresh water.

Local Indians burned that settlement to the ground and the colonists moved inland to the present site, at the confluence of the Tínima and Hatibonico Rivers.

There they felled trees for construction and used the local clay to make bricks, floor and roof tiles and giant *tinajones* — modeled on the big-bellied, wide-mouthed wine and oil jars from Spain — for collecting rainwater, since the area had practically no subsoil water. The size and number of *tinajones* a family possessed also came to be an indication of its economic status, though no household was without this essential utensil that identifies Camagüey even today.

In spite of its inland location, the villa was harassed by pirates. In 1668, Henry Morgan and his men raided and virtually destroyed the town. It was rebuilt in a web of tortuous streets with sharp turns and deadends that seem well suited to ambushes. Certainly the center city was not designed for cars and the best way to see it is to walk it.

Ignacio Agramonte's Birthplace opposite *Merced Church* (1748) at the edge of *Workers' Square* is a good place to start, for Camagüey's most famous son dominates the city's history. As the leader of Camagüey's rebel forces in Cuba's first War of Independence, Agramonte fought 45 battles before he fell in action on May 11, 1873.

Ignacio Agramonte was born December 23, 1841, in the second bedroom on the top floor where the family lived.

One of Camagüey's famous *tinajones*

The great parlor overlooking the street is furnished as it might have been in that period, though the only piece of family furniture is the piano that Amalia, Agramonte's young bride, played before the war of 1868 erupted and the family was dispersed. The size and number of *tinajones* in the ground floor interior patio of the Agramonte house attest to the family's wealth — as, of course, does the 18th-century mansion itself.

The Spanish colonial government immediately seized all the family's possessions, including the house. The top floor rooms were rented out and the ground floor became La Estrella, a tavern frequented by supporters of colonial rule. At the end of the war, the house was returned to members of the family and changed hands several times thereafter. La Estrella was replaced by the Correos Bar, the top floor became the Spanish Consulate during the early years of the Republic and the second floor was headquarters for the militant Street Vendors Union for some years. During the Batista dictatorship, young Camagüeyans met in the house to plan revolutionary actions.

Completely restored during the '70s, the mansion houses the *Provincial History Commission* as well as the museum that honors Ignacio Agramonte and shows how Camagüeyans of his class and period lived.

Other colonial points of interest are *La Soledad Church* with its frescoed interior, dating from 1775, and the lofty *Santa Iglesia Cathedral*, built in 1864, that faces *Ignacio Agramonte Park*. The *Ignacio Agramonte Provincial History Museum* on Ave. de los Mártires is housed in the old Spanish Cavalry Barracks. It includes archaeological, zoological, furniture and painting exhibits.

Camagüey's active cultural life is most dynamically represented by the fresh and vital *Camagüey Ballet*, whose choreography and style are distinct from the *National Ballet's*. The younger Camagüey company performs in its home town — usually in the splendid crystal and marble *Principal Theater*, built in 1850 — when it isn't on tour in Cuba or abroad. Local musicians — traditional and new troubadours — play and sing plaintive and provocative ballads at *La Casa de la Trova* (Troubadours' House), in a restored colonial mansion overlooking Agramonte Park.

There's enough to see and do to warrant at least a one-night stay in Camagüey. Tourist groups are usually bedded at the *Camagüey Hotel* on the Central Highway. The nearby town of Florida also has a modern three-star hotel on the Central Highway. And for those who prefer to be in the center of town, the smaller and older *Gran Hotel* at 67 Maceo Street is adequate except for the water situation.

SANTA LUCIA BEACH

From the provincial capital, a two-hour drive through fertile farm lands and small towns leads to lovely Santa Lucía Beach, 19 km. (12 mi.) of white sand and turquoise water on the north coast of Camagüey Province.

Santa Lucía is a favorite with Canadians who stay at the *Mayanabo Hotel*, an airy, two-story, three-wing, 225-room beach hotel, with a big swimming pool. At Mayanabo, guests can spend lazy hours around the pool or at the beach, doing water aerobics; snorkeling at the coral reef; horseback riding on the sand; biking to the local pizza parlor; stopping at the beach bar for a minty Mojito or a cold, strong *Tínima* beer, brewed in Camagüey; feasting on roast pork spitted by the hotel chef; sampling criollo specialties at nearby *Bahamas Restaurant;* tasting the fresh fish grilled to order at *Villa Tararaco* on down the beach; watching a dazzling musical show under the stars; or catching a video movie.

The Canadians buy a package that includes accommodations, one or two meals and a program of activities they can take or leave. Individual tourists visiting Santa Lucía during the winter season may find the Club Mayanabo — as its northern guests call it — booked to the last room. But Villa Tararaco has comfortable air-conditioned cabanas on the same beach.

Boats beached on
Santa Lucía

GUAIMARO

Just east of Camagüey on the Central Highway is the little
town of Guáimaro, where the Constitutional Assembly of
the Republic in Arms met in 1869 to hammer out basic policy for rebel-held territory. The men who attended that historic meeting were enlightened patriots, fighters for independence. But nothing they said or wrote during their sessions resounded with the import of what Ana Betancourt,
barred from the Assembly as a woman, said in Guáimaro's
public square:

"You fight for your country's freedom. You emancipate
your slaves. Now the time has come to liberate women."

Carlos Manuel de Céspedes hailed her as a woman
ahead of her time and Ignacio Agramonte urged the Assembly to support her plea. But though Article 24 of the
1869 Constitution stated "All inhabitants of the Republic
are completely free," it made no specific mention of
women's rights.

Born in 1832, Ana Betancourt fought for her country's
independence as well as women's suffrage. She conspired
and shared the vicissitudes of war with her husband Ignacio Mora. Together they edited the newspaper *El Mambí*
for the Camagüeyan troops and independence supporters.
Ana and Ignacio were ambushed in the battle zone, but she
managed to distract their captors until her husband es-

caped. Later, she too escaped, but was soon forced into exile. Ana never saw Ignacio again. He was captured and shot in 1875. She died in Madrid in 1901.

On the 150th anniversary of her birth, Ana Betancourt's ashes were brought from Madrid and deposited at the base of the monument erected in her honor outside the *Guáimaro History Museum*, the colonial building in which the 1869 Assembly was held.

Engraved on the monument are excerpts from her public speech: "In the obscurity and tranquility of the home, women have waited with patience and forbearance for this great moment when a new revolution would remove their yoke and free their wings. . . . " As the exhibits in the museum show, that new revolution finally triumphed in 1959 and only then were Ana Betancourt's demands met.

HOLGUIN PROVINCE

Next to Havana, Holguín is Cuba's most populous province — nearly a million inhabitants — and probably the most prosperous when the nickel around Moa and Nicaro, the world's largest reserves of this mineral, are weighed in with its agroindustrial production.

HOLGUIN

Over the past 20 years, Holguín, with a population of 240,640, has grown from a sleepy country town to a sprawling industrial city where, among other things, Cuba's big sugarcane harvesters are manufactured. The farm lands surrounding the city produce sugarcane and a wide variety of food products.

Colonial Center
In the central colonial part of the city, overlooking *Calixto García Park* — named for Holguín's best-known independence fighter — is the *Municipal Museum of History* in the

Holguín, colonial center

building historically known as *La Periquera* (Parrot Cage). It got its name because the Spanish soldiers billeted there, in their blue, yellow and green uniforms, looked like caged parrots behind the barred windows of the building when the rebels attacked it in 1868. The Museum's most important exhibit is the Holguín Ax, the 12-inch pre-Columbian figure of an elongated man carved in smoothly polished peridotic rock. Found in 1860 in the hills around Holguín, the ax is the provincial symbol and replicas of it are given as special achievement awards.

Also located on this square are the *Municipal Arts and Crafts Center*, the *Troubadours' House*, a gallery that exhibits local art and a number of stores. Just off the square, at 147 Miró Street, is the *Calixto García Birthplace-Museum*, an unpretentious country-style colonial house with exhibits relating to the General's life. A block away, on Maceo between Martí and Luz Caballero Streets, is the *Carlos de la Torre Museum of Natural History*, containing what is probably the finest collection of *polymita* shells in Cuba. These little snails with bright, variegated bands of yellow, red, green, purple, brown and white are found in trees and bushes along the coast of eastern Cuba. They were first identified and classified by Cuban naturalist Carlos de la Torre y Huerta, for whom the museum is named.

Should you happen to be in Holguín during annual Culture Week in mid-January, this area is the center of musical, theatrical, art and gastronomical happenings from afternoon to late evening.

Modern Rim

In a new neighborhood on the outskirts of the city, the marble mausoleum of Holguín's most famous son, backed by a huge frieze depicting heroic events and personages in Cuban history, is the focal point of *Calixto García Revolution Square*, where as many as 150,000 people gather for important rallies. In 1980, when the square was completed, García's remains were transferred from Havana for final burial there in his home town. From his mausoleum, a flagstone path leads back into the woods, to the grave of Lucía Iñiguez Landín, his patriotic mother. The bronze monument in her honor shows a Cuban flag hanging vertically behind her head, which is draped with a veil in the shape of Holguín Province. It is the custom for newlyweds to leave the bridal bouquet at the foot of the monument in remembrance of one who struggled for the freedom they now enjoy.

This is the area of Holguín where new apartment and office buildings, schools, polyclinics and hospitals, a big stadium and modern hotels have been built. In the latter category are the four-star *Pernik Hotel* — named for Bulgarian hero Georgi Dimitrov's birthplace and built with his country's aid — which has a marble lobby as big as a skating rink, 202 air-conditioned rooms with private baths, a restaurant, a cafeteria, a swimming pool and other facilities; and the more modest *El Bosque Motel:* 68 cabanas with private baths, a restaurant, a cafeteria, a pool and shops.

Mayabe Lookout

From the city, a short drive through rolling countryside brings you to *Mayabe Lookout* and a sweeping view of the valley, charming honeymoon cabanas, a beer-guzzling burro beside the swimming pool and an open-air, thatched-roof restaurant framed by purple bougainvillea and bright orange tulipán. The inside wall of the restaurant is covered with a woodburning of an Indian village which, like the ceramic tableware and raffia lampshades, was made by local artisans. The restaurant's succulent specialties are *fried chicken à la criollo* and *filete uruguayo* (steak stuffed with ham and cheese) — both moderately priced.

BARIAY NATIONAL PARK

From the picturesque fishing village of *Gibara* to the great *Bay of Nipe*, the northern shore of Holguín Province is a vast tourist reserve known as Bariay National Park, named for the beach where Christopher Columbus first landed in Cuba. This area includes some 35 beaches, the most famous of which is Guardalavaca,, as well as offshore cays, mountain caves and fertile farm land. During the next few years, new hotels and roads, beach facilities and an aquarium will be constructed as part of a development plan that calls for improvements at 88 sites in the area.

GUARDALAVACA BEACH

From a diaphanous blue sea, Guardalavaca's marine terrace rises to a 656-yard-long cushion of creamy white sand fringed by tropical shrubs. During the winter season, vacationers fly directly from Canada to the city of Holguín and continue by bus to Guardalavaca, some 54 km. (35 mi.) to the north, where they stay at the *Guardalavaca Hotel* (227 air-conditioned rooms with private baths) or the *Don Lino Club* (150 air-conditioned cabanas with private baths). Both these beach resorts have their own restaurants, bars, shops and recreational activities that include scuba diving at the six marked sites offshore. The hotel tourism bureaus offer a wide range of optional excursions. The new 230-room *Atlántico Norte Hotel*, now under construction, and the smaller villas and motels scheduled to be built within the next few years will have similar attractions.

Guardalavaca Beach on Holguín's north shore

GIBARA

Just 52 km. (34 mi.) west of Guardalavaca is the picturesque
fishing village of Gibara, with a population of 16,000. In addition to the fishing cooperative, the town has a spinning
mill; a shipyard; a 110-bed hospital with operating rooms,
labs and its own generating plant; schools; an ice factory
and water-filtering system; an Olympic-size swimming
pool; two hotels; two bookstores; two libraries; three
museums; and a community arts center. Some of Gibara's
historical buildings have recently been restored and others
— such as the battery, the military barracks and the Colonial Theater — soon will be.

On a guided tour of Gibara, visitors take in Gibara's
Colonial, History and *Natural History Museums* and stop for a
cool drink in a park overlooking the hospital, pool and
town beach. Then they continue to the fishing cooperative
where a seafood feast is served in a pink-and-white ginger-
bread social club that dates back to 1883. After lunch,
guests are escorted to the *Community Arts Center* to see a
local kiddy talent show before returning to the beach.

BARIAY BEACH

Near Gibara is *Bariay Beach,* with a monument marking Columbus' landing on October 26, 1492. Plans call for construction of a Taíno Indian village like the one Columbus
found there to mark the 500th anniversary of the Admiral's
"discovery" of America.

BANES

One of Cuba's most amazing indigenous art collections is
exhibited in the little town of Banes, a 40-minute drive
southeast of Guardalavaca Beach, where the unique
Museum of Indian Civilization is located.

Why there? Because 33 percent of Cuba's archaeological
wealth is located in Holguín Province and most of the digs

are in or around Banes, site of the pre-Columbian Bani Indian settlement. The Indian cemetery recently discovered in Chorro de Maíta near Banes is the largest known to exist in the Antilles and of particular interest as a point of contact between American and European cultures. The skeletons found there — all in good condition — included an Indian woman buried with lavish jewelry, two children adorned with European necklaces and bracelets and a Spaniard. Plans are to use one section of the cemetery as an archaeological museum.

Meanwhile, the existing museum in Banes exhibits some of the art and artifacts created by the Taíno Indian farmers and artisans who inhabited the area until the end of the 16th century. They used shells, rocks, bones, ceramics, wood and metal to fashion tools, utensils, figures, and jewelry related to their culture and customs. Incredibly, their work often seems more modern than art of a later period.

The museum's prize exhibit is a one-and-a-half-inch-high gold goddess — believed to date from the 13th century — wearing a feathered headdress and holding a bowl in offering. The theme of childbirth is depicted with moving realism in the ceramic figure of a woman in labor. Axes, bowls and other utensils are decorated with abstract designs and human forms. The handicrafts are so sophisticated they make you gasp. A necklace of graded symmetrical stones has a centerpiece with a delicate shell fossil embedded in it that would attract any fashion connoisseur's eye. Shells strung as belts, bracelets and necklaces would go well with today's casual clothes. A pendant with a man's head carved on one side and a woman's on the other speaks of mutual affection. The miniature Banes man and the tiny animals — some stone, others ceramic — are perfect in every detail.

There are also rocks with scenes or messages traced on both sides, apparently used to pass along information or describe rituals. José Martínez's wall murals depicting Indian life complement the exhibits in the museum's four rooms.

GRANMA PROVINCE

Granma Province, whose fields of sugarcane extend from its northern border with Las Tunas and Holguín to the slopes of the Sierra Maestra Mountains in the south, was created by the new political-administrative divisions of 1976. Before that, it was part of Oriente, province of history-making rebellion.

BAYAMO

You can ride through the streets of Bayamo in a horse-drawn carriage or in a brand new car. A carriage, though, is especially evocative of this city's past and it seems appropriate to ride that way into Bayamo's main square.

On one side of the square stands the splendid 18th-century house — now restored as a museum — where Carlos Manuel de Céspedes was born.

This man has gone down in history as the Father of the Country because he freed his slaves at *La Demajagua,* the sugar plantation he owned near Manzanillo, and declared Cuba's independence from Spain. The bold action of October 10, 1868, triggered a ten-year struggle for independence and was the climax of 15 years of conspiracy during which Céspedes was arrested several times because of his political ideas. During his imprisonment aboard a ship in Santiago de Cuba's harbor, he wrote articles on his favorite game, chess; and when he returned to Bayamo he established chess clubs there and in Manzanillo. On the eve of the war of 1868, Céspedes and his friends organized chess matches as a cover for their conspiratorial preparations.

Across the square from Céspedes birthplace is the Town Hall where, as President of the Republic of Cuba in Arms, he signed the document abolishing slavery in the liberated zones.

In the center of the square is a statue of Céspedes and a bust of another Bayamese patriot: "Perucho" Figueredo, who wrote the fighting march that is now Cuba's national anthem. It was first played in Bayamo's Mayor Parochial Church during Corpus Christi ceremonies on June 11, 1868, as the colonial governor of Bayamo listened in outraged astonishment. After the rebels took Bayamo and made it their capital, the march was sung openly in the square outside the church. A few months later, when reinforced Spanish troops tried to retake Bayamo, the rebels set the city on fire. They burned the church to the ground, but only after removing the intricately laminated wooden altar, which they hid until the war's end. It now occupies a nave in the rebuilt church located a block away from the main square.

Céspedes' birthplace survived the fire and successive owners. When Cuba attained its independence from Spain, local residents rounded up enough money to place a plaque on the facade commemorating the patriot's birth there on April 18, 1819. Then, for half a century, the building was used as the local post office. In 1968, on the centennial anniversary of La Demajagua Declaration of Independence, Céspedes' birthplace was opened as a museum.

The rooms off the red tile ground floor patio contain documents and photos tracing the history of Bayamo, the course of the War of Independence and Céspedes' principled life. When Spanish troops captured his son Oscar and proposed his surrender in return for the boy's life, the fighting President of the Republic in Arms rejected the proposal and Oscar was shot. When serious divisions within the revolutionary leadership led to his removal from the presidency, he retired without protest to the little town of

Céspedes' birthplace

San Lorenzo and awaited permission to leave the country so he could continue to aid the war from abroad. Meanwhile, he taught reading, writing . . . and chess. He had just finished a game of chess on February 24, 1874, when a battalion of Spanish troops raided the town and ordered Céspedes to surrender. Instead, he went down shooting, acting on the statement he had made earlier: "They can take me dead, but prisoner never."

Bayamo, of course, has fanned out from its main square into new commercial and residential districts. In one of these, on the Central Highway, is the four-star *Sierra Maestra Hotel*, with comfortable rooms and a restaurant where good food is served at an all too leisurely pace.

MANZANILLO

Manzanillo, Granma's second largest city, is a fishing port on the Gulf of Guacanayabo, for which the modern hotel that overlooks the harbor is named. The view from this hilltop hotel is matchless, especially early in the morning, when the sun strikes rooftops and sea with shafts of gold; or late on a velvety night, when twinkling lights in town and harbor rival the stars overhead. The three-star *Guacanayabo Hotel* has air-conditioned rooms with private baths; a swimming pool; a bar; a cafeteria; and a restaurant where service is at a snail's pace.

Sugar from the provincial mills is trucked or railed to Manzanillo for shipment by boat. On the city's railroad platform is a statue of Jesús Menéndez, the incorruptible sugar workers' leader who was assassinated there in 1948.

LA DEMAJAGUA

Just outside Manzanillo is the plantation, now a national park, where Céspedes freed his slaves and incorporated them into the ranks of his fighting troops. The freedom bell he rang that day hangs in the recess of the plantation stone wall, as it did then. The farm buildings hold archaeological and historical exhibits and many of Céspedes' personal effects.

MEDIA LUNA

The coastal highway connecting Manzanillo with Niquero, the province's second port, runs past fields of sugarcane and through small towns named Campechuela, San Ramón and Media Luna (Half Moon) where the late Celia Sánchez Manduley, heroine of the Sierra Maestra and the triumphant revolution, was born on May 9, 1920. Growing up in sugar-producing Media Luna, where her father was the local doctor and a follower of Martí, Celia learned early about poverty, exploitation and struggle. In 1953, to commemorate the centenary anniversary of Martí's birth, Celia and Dr. Manuel Sánchez Silveira placed a bust of the Apostle on Turquino Peak, the highest point in the Sierra Maestra. From then until she joined the rebel forces in the mountains, Celia was involved in propaganda, liaison and clandestine rebel actions of all kinds. Shortly after her death in 1980, a contingent of the Venceremos Brigade — composed of US citizens who show their support of Cuba through annual work trips to the island — passed through Media Luna while touring this historic part of Cuba and planted a mahogany tree in Celia's memory in the back yard of the Sánchez house. The tree has thrived and so has Celia's birthplace, now a museum that nurtures the kinds of community cultural and educational activities she considered so important.

LAS COLORADAS BEACH

On the southwest coast of the province, 20 km. (12 mi.) beyond the port of Niquero, is Las Coloradas Beach, the inhospitable swampland where the 26th of July expeditionaries beached the *Granma* on December 2, 1956, when they returned from Mexico to start guerrilla warfare in the Sierra Maestra Mountains. A wooden pathway has been built across the murky terrain they had to forge on foot. Beside it is a monument in a square where as many as 15,000 people can gather for rallies and meetings.

MAREA DEL PORTILLO BEACH

From Media Luna, a road forks southeast through hilly country with an occasional glimpse of the sea. Unexpectedly, just before the blacktop mountain road ends at the foot of the Sierra Maestra Mountains, a tree-lined lane leads off to the right toward a small Caribbean bay with a black sand beach partially shaded by palm trees: Marea del Portillo.

At the edge of the beach is the low-rise, low-key hotel surrounded by tropical vegetation, exuding casual relaxation. The hotel has 74 air-conditioned rooms with private baths, telephone and radio; a wood-paneled dining room cooly decorated in blue and white; a large hexagonal pool with plenty of lounge space around it; an open-sided snack bar and game room just beyond the pool; outside sports facilities; and a thatched-roof snack bar on the sparkling black sand beach. During the winter tourist season, Canadians fly by direct charter from Toronto to Manzanillo and

Marea del Portillo Beach

Horseback riding into the Sierra Maestra from the Marea del Portillo Hotel

continue by bus to the *Marea del Portillo Hotel* for one- or two-week vacations. During the summer, it is used by other foreign visitors and Cubans.

SIERRA MAESTRA NATIONAL PARK

All along the coast eastward from Marea del Portillo, the mountains rise majestically through Granma, Santiago de Cuba and Guantánamo Provinces.

This rugged terrain with its exceptional flora and fauna was the camping ground and battlefield for the guerrilla war waged against Batista's troops from 1956 to 1959 and it is filled with the evidence of that struggle: at *La Plata*, where the Rebel Army established its General Headquarters; and at rural outposts such as *El Uvero, Pino del Agua* and *Jigüe*, where the rebels won decisive victories. New roads provide access to these history-making spots and also give visitors a chance to see the mountain schools, houses, farm cooperatives and clinics built in recent years. And even in the most remote areas, you're likely to meet a community doctor making his rounds and treating his patients, since the mountains have priority in Cuba's nation-wide family doctor health care program.

SANTIAGO DE CUBA PROVINCE

From Granma Province, the Sierra Maestra Mountains hug the Caribbean coast all the way to the city of Santiago de Cuba, then jut north toward Holguín and east to Guantánamo. Sugarcane covers the plains in the northwest, but the rest of Santiago de Cuba Province is mountainous and sparsely populated, with coffee plantations clinging to forested slopes.

SANTIAGO DE CUBA

At the foot of the mountains lies Santiago de Cuba, the island's second largest city, with a population of over 340,000 and a cultural mix that gives it a cosmopolitan air. Santiago is the country's "most Caribbean city" — as well as the "cradle of the revolution" and Cuba's only officially designated Hero City.

Santiago is also warm, hospitable and thoroughly enchanting. Viewed from the radiant bay, the city seems to rise on natural terraces crowded with houses that project lacy grillwork, turned wooden balustrades, forged iron railings, hanging balconies and narrow outside staircases.

Entering the city along the Central Highway, you hover above it at the *University of Oriente* — its *Archaeological Museum* shows interesting facets of Cuban Indian culture — and nearby *El Rancho Motel* (29 air-conditioned cabanas with private baths, restaurant-cabaret, bar and shops).

Moncada

Descending gradually, the highway crosses Trinidad Street at the site of the **26th of July School City**, the former **Moncada Garrison** that Fidel Castro and his rebel group attacked on July 26, 1953.

The Moncada was Cuba's second largest garrison and the plan was to seize it by surprise and call for a people's uprising. The heroic attack failed but it provided the moral

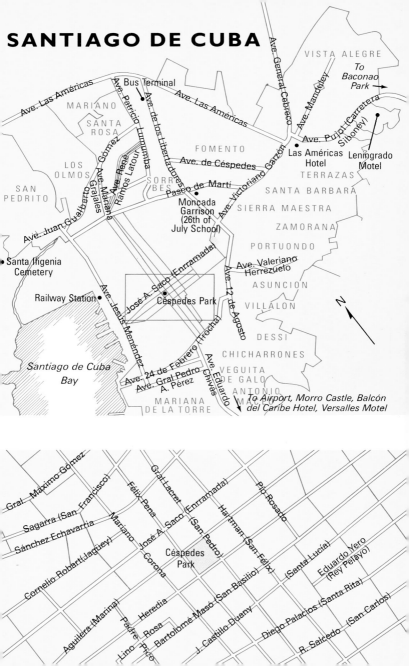

SANTIAGO DE CUBA

VISTA ALEGRE

To Baconao Park →

Ave. General Cebreco

Ave. Las Américas

Bus Terminal

MARIANO

SANTA ROSA

Ave. Las Américas

Ave. de los Libertadores

Ave. Patricio Lumumba

Ave. Mandeley

Ave. Pujol (Carretera Siboney)

Las Américas Hotel

Leningrado Motel

LOS OLMOS

Gómez

Ave. René Ramos Latour

FOMENTO

Ave. de Céspedes

TERRAZAS

SAN PEDRITO

Ave. Mariana Grajales

SORRIBES

Paseo de Martí

SANTA BARBARA

SIERRA MAESTRA

Ave. Juan Gualberto

Ave. Victoriano Garzón

Moncada Garrison (26th of July School)

ZAMORANA

PORTUONDO

Santa Ifigenia Cemetery

Ave. Jesús Menéndez

José A. Saco (Enrramada)

Ave. Valeriano Herrezuelo

ASUNCION

Railway Station

Ave. 12 de Agosto

Céspedes Park

VILLALON

DESSI

N

CHICHARRONES

Santiago de Cuba Bay

Ave. 24 de Febrero (Trocha)

Ave. Gral Pedro A. Pérez

Ave. Eduardo Chivás

VEGUITA DE GALO

ANTONIO

MARIANA DE LA TORRE

To Airport, Morro Castle, Balcón del Caríbe Hotel, Versalles Motel →

Gral. Máximo Gómez

Grat Lacret

Félix Pena

José A. Saco (Enrramada)

Pío Rosado

Sagarra (San Francisco)

Mariano Corona

Hartman (San Félix)

Sánchez Echavarria

Cornelio Robart (Jaguey)

Céspedes Park

(Santa Lucía)

Eduardo Yero (Rey Pelayo)

Aguilera (Marina)

Heredia

Padre Rosa

Lino Pico

Bartolomé Masó (San Básilio)

J. Castillo Duany

Diego Palacios (Santa Rita)

R. Salcedo (San Carlos)

base for the 26th of July Movement and its Rebel Army which — with tremendous popular backing — overthrew the Batista dictatorship on January 1, 1959, and set Cuban history on a new course. On January 28, 1960, the 107th anniversary of Martí's birth, the former military stronghold became a school with an enrollment of more than 2000 students. One wing, where bullet holes are still visible, was turned into a museum that traces Cuba's freedom struggles and shows some of the advances made since the triumph of the revolution. *Like most museums in Santiago, this one is open Tuesday through Saturday from 8 a.m. to noon and 2 to 6 p.m. and on Sunday morning. You can verify museum visiting hours at the hotel tourism bureau.*

Céspedes Park

Santiago's streets form a special urbanistic design, some leading in toward the mountains and others out to the coast, all apparently emanating from **Céspedes Park.** Showcase, mirror and heart of the city, the park has a monument to Carlos Manuel de Céspedes at its center. The splendid buildings around the square are best viewed from the rooftop terrace cabaret of the old *Casagranda Hotel*. (The Santiago tourism office in the basement makes hotel reser-

Cathedral,
Céspedes Square

vations, books excursions and provides information about
what's happening in the city.)

To the left of the Casagranda is the *Cathedral*, built in
1523, with the Angel of the Annunciation above the por-
tals. The Cathedral's *Ecclesiastical Museum* has interesting
documents and objects related to the Catholic Church of
Santiago. On the same side of the square are the *Gallery of
Oriente Art*, where local artists exhibit their works; and the
Arts and Crafts Shop that sells the wonderful creations of
Santiago's artisans.

Straight across the park is a mansion with a plateresque
stone facade and dark, Moorish balconies overhanging the
street, their closed shutters guarding mysteries within.
Built between 1516 and 1530, it is the oldest house in Cuba
and its pre-baroque architecture is more severe than the
neo-classical addition to it constructed between 1800 and
1810. In the 16th century, Governor Diego Velázquez lived
there, using the ground floor for his House of Commerce
and Gold Foundry and the upstairs as living quarters. At
the rear of the interior patio is the foundry furnace, somewhat damaged by time. In later years, the building became
a hotel, a Masonic Club and an office building before it was
restored and opened as the *Museum of Colonial Art*.

The spacious rooms with elaborately decorated ceilings
and gleaming tile floors contain furniture, tapestries, crystal, ceramics, lamps and art work that belonged to members of Santiago's colonial ruling class. The spacious family
rooms, shuttered for privacy, give the house a certain timeless impenetrability that is in tranquil contrast to the color,
rhythm and music just outside.

Cultural Feast

Heredia Street is a vibrant arm extending out of Céspedes
Park and the scene of a three-block cultural fiesta held
every Saturday and Sunday from 7:30 p.m. on. These Cultural Nights on Heredia Street act like a magnet, drawing
people from everywhere. Traffic is blocked off so folks can
wander all over the street, looking in on this or that attrac-

Downtown Santiago

tion, stopping to watch puppeteers, mimes, clowns, magicians, musicians, dancers, actors.

Traditional songsters arrive at the *Troubadours' House,* guitars in hand. There, in the bohemian setting of a small parlor that opens directly onto the street, these eternally inspired poets of the night serenade — and jam — for hours.

Next door, the *Student Center* is filled with the colorful syncopation young *santiagueros* love. At the corner, *El Cocal* serves strong drinks and *prú,* a soft drink made with pepper leaves, vanilla, pine needles, soapberries and India root. Across the street, the *House of Cheese* sells Guaicanamar, Gorgonzola, Pigmée, Cuban Camembert and Carré de l'Est cheeses, cider, wines and beer.

Further along is the birthplace — now a museum — of *José María Heredia,* the first Cuban poet to extol liberation, In the *Elvira Cape Library* is a lyrical corner where opera lovers can listen to recorded arias and duets sung by the immortals. In a small theater, *Cabildo Teatral* presents comedy or drama.

At the imposing *Union of Writers and Artists of Cuba (UNEAC),* poets read their verses in the patio while artists interpret their paintings and sculptures exhibited in the front gallery. Next comes the *Carnival Museum,* a tribute to centuries of the festive soul of Santiago. Another surprise is *Tango Circle,* featuring the popular melodies of that genre amidst hats and scarves reminiscent of the great Carlos Gardel. Back in the street, *La Tumba Francesa* and the *Folklore Group* perform ancestral expressions of Afro-Cuban dance and song.

People are everywhere: happy, relaxed, walking arm in arm, dancing, singing. Much of the crowd spills into *Enramada Street,* a block away, where vendors vie with art and entertainment by setting up their kiosks and stands to sell arts and crafts, birds, books, clothing, cosmetics, flowers, toys — and the tantalizing street food that necessarily accompanies such fiestas.

Santiago Carnival

Only at **Carnival** during July does the tempo of Santiago rise above the relaxed beat of these cultural nights. Anyone visiting Santiago then is literally swept along with the Carnival, dancing a street rumba, joining a snaking conga line, downing shots of rum and succumbing to the frenzied rhythm of drums. Nowhere else in Cuba is Carnival such a people's fiesta; and nowhere else are the *comparsas* or street dances more varied and traditional.

Santiago Carnival would be inconceivable without the *Carabalí* street dances that have launched these festivities since the 19th century. *Carabalí Izuama* is the oldest group, founded by two brothers who became majors in Cuba's War of Independence, and *Carabalí Olugo* is a later offshoot of the original group. The *Carabalís* wear the court attire of 19th-century Spain, but their dances and music — played with a snare and a bass drum, a fife, a *melé* and maracas — are pure African.

La Tumba Francesa is another well-known group. This society was founded in 1862 by Haitian émigrés and has retained the original *yubá, masón, cobrero* and *tahona* rhythms characterized by elegance and strong cadence.

These and other street dance groups have their own studios where they rehearse two or three times a week all year long and welcome anyone who wants to drop in and watch. *Carabalí Izuama* is on Pío Rosado between Los

Maceo and San Antonio Streets, *Carabalí Olugo* is at 496 Trocha Street and *La Tumba Francesa* is at 501 Los Maceo (corner of San Bartolomé). *All three groups rehearse Tuesdays and Fridays at 8:30 p.m.*

Taking It All In

For an overall view of the history of eastern Cuba, a visit to the *Emilio Bacardí Museum*, located on Pío Rosado between Heredia and Aguilera Streets, is a must. Founded in 1899 by Emilio Bacardí Moreau, patriot, writer and de facto Mayor of Santiago, the museum is Cuba's oldest. It contains documents, banners, weapons, work tools and personal effects of almost all the great independence fighters; archaeological findings; an Egyptian mummy; European paintings; and an important archives section.

Just off Céspedes Park, at the corner of Aguilera and Calvario Streets, *La Isabelica Coffee Shop* beckons with the aroma of the black nectar mixed with creams, liqueurs, rum or fruit. For a full meal — in the salon of a charming colonial house in the center city — the elegant *1900 Restaurant*, on San Basilio between Pío Rosado and Hartman Streets, is made to order. Once you're past the stuffed St. Bernard dog and iron jockey that guard the entrance hall, you can enjoy the crystal chandeliered dining room with its antique furnishings; the dinner music played by a trio on piano, bass fiddle and drum; and the excellent, moderately priced meal: beef steak at $7.50, turkey or rabbit at $5.50 (prices subject to change, of course). *The 1900 Restaurant is open Tuesday through Sunday from noon to 3 p.m. and 7 to 11 p.m. Advance reservations are advisable.*

Everyone in Santiago agrees that *Padre Pico* is the city's most picturesque street, a broad stone stairway with precariously perched houses on both sides. Climb it to the top — or circle the hill by road and look down the steps from the corner of Santa Rita Street, where the *Museum of the Underground Struggle* is located. During the November 30, 1956 uprising, a 26th of July commando firebombed the Batista police headquarters housed in this building. The museum pays tribute to the martyrs of that and other actions in the underground struggle.

Antonio Maceo Grajales, the Bronze Titan of Cuba's War of Independence, was born in a modest house on the street renamed Los Maceo for his family. Built between 1800 and 1830, the house has the fiber walls commonly used to miti-gate damage from earthquakes, wood paneled floors and a tile roof. The living room is devoted to Maceo's military feats, from his first battle in 1868, to his final battle and death on December 7, 1896. In the room where he was born are exhibits relating to his personal life, including photos of the 21-year-old Antonio and his young bride María Ca-brales Fernández. In a third room are examples of Maceo's anti-imperialist, anti-racist and patriotic thinking.

The birthplace of *Frank and Josué País,* two young martyrs from a later phase of Cuba's freedom struggle, is also a museum, located at 266 General Bandera between Trinidad and Habana Streets. Frank País, poet, teacher and National Action Leader of the 26th of July Movement, led the San-tiago uprising of November 30, 1956, planned in coordina-tion with the *Granma* landing, then reorganized the under-ground movement in support of the guerrilla front in the mountains. Frank's younger brother Josué, also active in the Movement, was killed in a shootout in June 1957 and Frank was assassinated by police agents a month later, on July 30.

The *Santa Ifigenia Cemetery,* on Ave. de las Américas north of the center city, is the final resting place for many of Cuba's patriots. José Martí, Carlos Manuel de Céspedes and Frank País are buried there. Martí's white marble mauso-leum has been placed so that the sun always falls on it.

The Morro of Santiago

As it has for centuries, Santiago's **Morro Castle**, San Pedro de la Roca, dominates sea and city from its craggy site at the mouth of the bay. Completed in 1710, its solid construc-tion and strategic location saved it from attack, though the ravages of time and weather eventually took a heavy toll.

After a long period of neglect, the fortress was painstakingly restored and reopened in 1978. Drawbridges protect entrances that open through thick walls into a labyrinth of passages and staircases, ramps and rooms. Through apertures for gun emplacements, a sudden light from the sea pierces the shadows. Patios hold powder magazines and a tread to lift the cannonballs to their loading point. Low-ceiling cells have built-in iron rings for shackling slaves and prisoners. The barracks seems inadequate for quartering more than a handful of soldiers. Near it is a small chapel with straight-backed wooden benches, its walls bare except for a large wooden cross bearing the figure of Christ carved by an anonymous Spanish artist.

In the Morro is the *Piracy Museum*, which, as the introductory plaque says "traces the most significant incidents of piracy in two important historical periods." The first period covers the corsairs and pirates of the 16th through 19th centuries while the second is devoted to examples of imperialist piracy against Latin-American nations from 1900 to the present. The Piracy Museum is strong stuff indeed: a history of the region's evolution as seen by a David who fought Goliath and won.

Santiago's Morro Castle

Cayo Granma

In the middle of the bay off the Morro Castle lies **Cayo Granma**, a one-hill islet reached by ferry from the Tourist Highway that hugs the coast. Formerly called Cayo Smith after its wealthy owner, it was then a vacation resort for those who could afford to build — or rent — summer houses on the slopes above the shore where poor fishermen lived. More than the name has changed since then, for Cayo Granma has a school, a polyclinic, stores and restaurants for the regular folks who live there now: some 4000 commuters who work in Santiago and a handful of fishermen and service employees. With all its advances, Cayo Granma retains a quaint charm in the mix of old and new single-family houses; the promenade that circles an islet where bicycles and carts are the only means of transportation; the restful isolation of Socapa Beach, on the other side of the island from the ferry landing; the miniature square just above the wharf; and the fresh seafood served at the little *Mar Azul Restaurant* that overlooks the Bay and the mighty Morro Castle on the far shore.

On the Santiago coast a few steps away from the Morro is the *San Pedro del Mar Restaurant-Cabaret*, which specializes in roast pork and offers a nightly show. On the coast next to it is the three-star *Balcón del Caribe Hotel* (92 air-conditioned rooms with private baths and its own restaurant, bar, cabaret, swimming pool and shops). These installations are some 7 km. outside the city.

Perched on a hill somewhat closer to the city, on the road leading to the airport, are the leafy terraces of the *Versalles Motel* (91 air-conditioned rooms with private baths, refrigerators, TVs, telephones and radios; also a restaurant, a bar, a cabaret, a cafeteria, a swimming pool and shops).

Las Américas Hotel (65 air-conditioned rooms with private baths, two restaurants, cafeteria, bar and shop), at Las Américas Avenue and General Cebreco, has an urban setting and is closer in than the others, though not really downtown. The center city hotels are old and generally seedy — remodeling is a promise for the future.

DOS RIOS

Northwest of Santiago, at the convergence of the Cauto and Contramaestre Rivers, is the small town of Dos Ríos where José Martí was killed in combat on May 19, 1895, three months after he had landed to launch Cuba's second War of Independence. A monument marks the spot where he fell.

EL COBRE

El Cobre, 16 km. (12 mi.) northwest of Santiago, is named for the first open copper mine in the Americas, which Indians, free blacks and slaves began working there in 1550; revered for its precious mestizo image of the *Virgen de la Caridad del Cobre,* brought to the town in 1608 and declared patron saint of Cuba in 1916; and remembered for one of the biggest slave rebellions in Cuba's history, in 1731.

By the early years of the 17th century, under the efficient management of Artillery Captain Francisco Sánchez Moya, the copper mine was producing enough to satisfy the needs of Havana's Artillery Works and the town was prosperous and peaceful, with a new church presided over by three recognized saints:

Miracles

One fine morning in 1608, the Indian brothers Juan and Rodrigo de Hoyos and a 10-year-old slave called Juan Moreno were collecting salt for the copper miners at the Bay of Nipe when, from their small boat, they spotted something floating in the water. According to the testimony Juan Moreno gave 75 years later, they marveled when the object turned out to be a foot-tall wooden statue of Mary carrying the Christchild on her left arm and holding a gold cross in her right hand. Supporting the image was a board bearing the inscription: "Yo soy la Virgen de la Caridad" (I am the Virgin of Charity).

Since the main altar of the recently built town church was already occupied by the powerful Santiago el Mayor and the side altars by Santa Barbara and Nuestra Señora del Rosario, a palm-thatched shrine was built for the Virgin outside the town. But the Virgin, it seemed, was determined to be in El Cobre: according to the solemnly sworn statements of the Hoyos brothers, she disappeared on three successive nights and was found, each time, at the top of a hill in Cobre. Half convinced of the Virgin's miraculous powers, Sánchez Moya built a chapel for her next to the main church in El Cobre.

In 1620, Sánchez Moya relinquished management of the mine, the church and 200 miners to Captain Juan de Eguiluz and returned to Spain. After Eguiluz's death ten years later, mining was virtually abandoned and the slaves, in effect, became free, though their ownership technically reverted to the Crown.

Meanwhile, belief in the Virgin's miraculous powers continued to spread and, when the second church was erected in El Cobre at the beginning of the 18th century, the Virgin de la Caridad rather than Santiago occupied the main altar.

Rebellion

El Cobre was a town of faith, freedom and peace until, in 1731, Colonel Don Pedro Giménez, Governor of Santiago, ordered the copper mine reopened with the forced labor of the descendants of Eguiluz's slaves. But those descendants defended their freedom with machetes and muskets in one of the island's biggest slave insurrections. And apparently the Virgin sided with the insurgents, for instead of a confrontation there was mediation through the Bishop of Santiago; and, after promises, delays and evasions, El Cobre's 1065 descendants of slaves were declared free by Royal Decree in 1782. Eventually, in 1830, the mine was successfully reactivated — with free labor — and continued to produce until its best ore had been extracted in the 20th century.

El Cobre Basilica, main entrance

The Virgin and the Basilica

Through the years, the Virgin has been invoked to protect freedom, perform miracles, offer consolation and heal the bitterness of battle. In 1916, at the petition of veterans of the War of Independence, the Pope declared her the patron saint of Cuba. She was transferred to her present home in El Cobre's third church on her saint's day, September 8, 1927, and coronated with a jeweled crown on September 8, 1936.

Her temple — a cream-colored, red-domed rectangle with bougainvillea bushes flaming between each of the Stations of the Cross along its outside wall — stands on a hill overlooking the town and the mine. Its status as Cuba's only Basilica was officially celebrated on May 7, 1978.

The church nave rises in arched vaults above stained-glass windows set high in the side walls. Almost at the top of the wall to the right of the altar is the air-conditioned niche containing the diminutive, aloof figure of the Virgin.

Dressed in a creamy satin, gold-encrusted gown, a gold cape over her shoulders and a replica of the valuable crown on her head, the Virgin presides over a little shrine at which people customarily leave flowers. On her saint's day, a church warden presses an electric button that turns the Virgin around to face the multitude assembled before the altar to hear mass.

Replicas of the dark-skinned saint are displayed in churches all over the island and La Virgen de la Caridad Church in Havana is named for her. She is usually shown rising on the waves, with the three salt collectors gazing at her in awe from their little boat. At the Basilica, she stands alone — for she arrived at El Cobre before the miracle of her discovery had spread.

The Virgin de la Caridad del Cobre is truly a saint for all believers: in the syncretism of Cuban Catholicism and African religious rites, her Yoruba name is Ochún, a powerfully magnetic goddess of *santería* who is also representative of so many Cuban women "in her sensual grace and criollo charm," as folklorist Miguel Barnet has noted.

The Basilica is open from 6 a.m. to noon and 1 to 5:45 p.m. and services are held every day. Behind the Basilica is the modest hotel run by church officials, where a hot meal costs about four pesos and rooms are priced at $7 for doubles and $3.50 for singles.

BACONAO PARK

San Juan Hill

At Km. 1 on the Siboney Highway east of Santiago is the *Leningrado Motel*, built around the little Spanish fortress at the foot of *San Juan Hill*, where the final battle of Cuba's War of Independence was fought. At the entrance is the huge ceiba tree under which the Spanish troops surrendered to US troops on July 16, 1898, in a ceremony from which Major General Calixto García, commander of the Cuban troops, was barred. The ground floor of the fortress now has a restaurant, a cafeteria, a bar and shops that open onto a great patio-cabaret. Behind this building, 32 two-story cabanas (with air-conditioning, private baths, TVs, radios and telephones) are scattered over shady grounds near the Olympic-size swimming pool.

At the top of San Juan Hill, bronze statues of a Cuban Mambí independence fighter and an American Rough Rider commemorate those who died in the Spanish-American War. On the other side of the hill, as far as the eye can see, the *26th of July Amusement Park* offers rides and games, interspersed with snack bars and cafeterias.

This is the beginning of Baconao Park, nearly 200,000 acres of land stretching out between the Caribbean and the Sierra Maestra from Santiago to Guantánamo.

Gran Piedra

From the Siboney Highway, a road winds up the wooded mountains to *Gran Piedra*, a huge glacial rock balanced 1000 m. (3300 ft.) above sea level, from which you can see Haiti and Jamaica on a clear day. *La Piedra Motel*, the mountain-top tourist installation, has 22 modern cabanas, a restaurant, a cafeteria and a bar. Nearby, one of the ruined coffee plantations that Haitian émigrés established in the 18th century has been restored as *La Isabelica Museum*.

Granjita Siboney

The *Granjita Siboney*, 12 km. (7 mi.) outside Santiago on the Siboney Highway, is the little farm that served as headquarters and point of departure for the attack on the Moncada Garrison. The farmhouse is now a museum exhibiting uniforms, weapons and personal possessions of the rebels, as well as newspaper accounts of the attack and the subsequent torture and murder of 68 of the captured men. All along the road to the farm are simple monuments, each bearing the name and occupation of a fighter who died in the Moncada action.

Balneario del Sol
Hotel terrace

Caribbean coast in
Baconao Park

Along the Coast

Near the entrance to the park is *Archaeological Valley*, with
its lifesize reproductions of prehistoric animals. Park facilities range from campsites (*Los Cactus* is one) and attractive
cabanas (as at *Verraco Beach*) to *Balneario del Sol*, a luxurious
new hotel complex with a crystal clear natural swimming
pool extending across the entire front of its seaside promenade. Local artists designed the one-of-a-kind wall hang-
ings, lamps, statues and other original objects that decorate the
thatched-roof restaurant, the grounds and the hotel itself.

Two of the best restaurants in Baconao Park are located
across from each other, at *Sigua Beach*: just off the road is
the famous *Casa de Pedro el Cojo* (Lame Peter's House),
specializing in criollo dishes — from the road you catch a
tantalizing whiff of roast pork — and above it, on a cliff
overlooking the sea, is *Los Corales*, which serves deliciously
fresh seafood.

Baconao Park also has cactus gardens; black, gold and
white sand beaches; inland lakes; scuba sites; fairgrounds;
seaside apartments; trails into the wilderness; kiddy rides;
snack bars; pools; aquariums; and zoos between the blue
Caribbean and the green-robed Sierra Maestra. This national park is still being developed as one of Cuba's great
vacation resorts and new installations appear all the time,
blending into a landscape that nature dominates.

GUANTANAMO PROVINCE

Flat and desert-like along the southern coast, Guantánamo
Province is mountainous to the north and east, with broad
rivers running down to the sea. The province grows sugarcane, coffee, cacao, coconuts and bananas.

GUANTANAMO

Most of Cuba's salt is produced in the city of Guantánamo,
though it is probably best known for its proximity to the US
Naval Base, maintained against the will of the government
and people of Cuba. The provincial capital has few tourist
attractions, but the unusual *Stone Zoo* in nearby Yateras
Municipality is well worth a visit. It has nearly a hundred
individual animals carved out of huge blocks of local limestone by Angel Iñigo, a self-trained artist from the area.

The *Guantánamo Hotel* in the provincial capital is a comfortable stopover for the road-weary traveler and a good
place to eat. For a typically Cuban meal of roast pork, *congrí*
and all the trimmings, the open, thatched-roof restaurant
at the *Motel Hanoi* is your choice.

BARACOA

Cuba's earliest settlement (1512), first capital (1512-15) and
easternmost city remains as unspoiled as it was in 1492,
when Columbus marveled at its rivers, bays and beaches,
its terraces rising steeply from the shore and the ''high,
square mountain that looks like an island,'' as the Admiral
described the anvil-shaped *El Yunque.*

For four and a half centuries after Columbus disem-
barked and planted a huge cross on land in the name of
God and the Queen of Spain, immigrants, pirates, fishermen, traders and visitors continued to reach Baracoa by
sea, for no roads were built to connect this outpost with the
rest of Cuba until after the triumph of the revolution. Now
you can drive from Guantánamo through desert-like flat-

Stone Zoo

lands and then across *La Farola* (Beacon), a 30 km. (20 mi.) scenic roller coaster highway constructed in the early '60s that spirals up through precipitous green peaks and deep ravines and down the northern slopes of the Cuchillas de Baracoa Mountains to the *Bahía de Miel* (Bay of Honey) at the entrance to the city.

Baracoa has mile after mile of virgin beaches stretching out all along the northeastern coast back to the Yumurí River and, on the northwestern shore, from Duaba Beach — where a simple obelisk marks the point at which General Antonio Maceo landed in 1895 to do battle with the Spanish colonial army — to the mouth of the great Toa River and on to virgin Maguana Beach, midway between Baracoa and Moa. Behind the beaches rise El Yunque, the Sleeping Beauty and other mountains that have sheltered perse-cuted Indians, runaway slaves and rebel fighters in a wilderness of varied flora and fauna, caves, winding trails and pre-Columbian archaeological treasures that now lure both nature lovers and scientists.

The Fortresses

In the 18th century, when Baracoa assumed considerable strategic importance, three major fortifications were built to protect it. *Fort Matachín,* on the northeastern coast, over-looks the Bay of Honey at the entrance to the city. On the northwestern coast, *La Punta* surveys the port. *El Castillo* — or Seboruco or Sanguily, as it has also been called — is embedded in the rocky summit of the 40-m. (132 ft.) marine terrace that rises sharply a few blocks in from the shore, commanding the port, the bay and the heart of the city. All three have been restored and are now used for other purposes.

Matachín Municipal Museum retains the original mortar walls, brick floors and even the little bunker that has an ingenious air circulation system designed to keep the gunpowder dry; but it has probably seen more action since its inauguration as a museum in October 1981 than it did in its 200 years as a fort, for it has become the research and documentation center for Baracoa's history and archaeological digs as well as a vital and mobile educational institution. The museum's chronologically arranged exhibits lead off with Taíno Indian artifacts — fragments of pottery, jewelry and cooking utensils, including a valuable pestle found intact in the area — and continue to the present. Two blocks inland from Matachín is the little tower the Spanish officers maintained as a checkpoint to keep Baracoans from smuggling supplies and arms to the rebels in the hills.

La Punta's lookout fort was built with a secret boat slip for dispatching messengers to the port. Later, it seemed only natural that the city's radio-telegraph station should be established there. Its austere, semi-circular walls now enclose a restaurant-cabaret with an open-air dance floor.

El Castillo is an impressive fortress reached by a winding driveway or a steep 85-step stone staircase cut into the sheer face of the cliff. Beside the cannon-flanked tower entrance to the fortress, a wall plaque credits the infamous US General Leonard Wood with remodeling the fort in 1905. In the latest remodeling, El Castillo has become a colonial-style hotel with 23 air-conditioned rooms and private baths. A glass-paneled restaurant-bar now extends from the kitchen out into the gardens, the only addition to the fortress. The hotel food is always good and a dinner serenade by Los Yunqueños Trio adds to the pleasure. El Castillo is an exceptionally clean and comfortable hotel with a spectacular view of mountains, harbor and city — a real find at ten pesos a day.

The Malecón

Baracoa's *Malecón* seaside drive is the third longest in Cuba, outdistanced only by those in Havana and Cienfuegos. It starts at *La Playita,* the gaily parasoled town beach next to Matachín, and ends at La Punta. In between, *El Caracol Restaurant* serves fresh lobster enchilada accompanied by delicately fried ripe bananas. Sturdy wooden tables and benches and the *polymita* shell lamps for which the restaurant is named give the place a casual, rustic air. *Los Románticos Trio* provides the musical ambience for a pleasant meal. Nearby is *La Rusa Hotel*, originally owned by a Russian woman who fled to Cuba after the revolution in her own country and built the boarding house where she lived until her death in 1979.

The Flavor of Baracoa

Baracoa has a history and a flavor all its own. Its residents debate whether or not the so-called *Cross of Parra* is the one Columbus brought ashore, though everyone agrees the relic is much older than the 19th-century Cathedral where

Baracoa

it is protected from the whittlers who cut away so many slivered blessings over the years. Visitors can't help but be enthralled by Baracoa's unique zoo, started by the man everyone calls *el rubio* (though his hair is red rather than blonde). The zoo's prize exhibit is the nearly extinct *almiquí*, a 400,000-year-old rodent-like mammal indigenous to eastern Cuba. In the heart of the city is the small, wooden *Troubadours' House*, where guitarists play in friendly competition; and the grandly colonial *Community Arts Center*, where you may catch dancers doing *el nengen* fox-trot and *el kiriba* polka, Baracoan adaptations of the famous Cuban *son*. Then there are the craftsmen who create precious wood carvings, seed pictures, bead curtains, shell lampshades, fiber baskets and pottery in the *Baracoa Arts and Crafts Workshop*; or do it on their own, like Pelayo Alvarez López, whose house at 25 Félix Ruenes Street is a museum filled with the furniture he has made of majagua, cedar and other woods, some inlaid with mother-of-pearl.

Even the food is different in Baracoa. In season — beginning seven days after the August full moon and extending into December — Baracoans bring out nets, sieves or cloths to catch *tetí*, the small red fish that arrive in a gelatinous ball at the mouth of the *Toa River*, then break apart on contact with fresh water and swim frantically upstream. *Tetí* is eaten raw with a cocktail sauce, turned into an omelette or an enchilada or fried lightly and mixed with rice. Another favorite dish is *bacán*, made of grated banana and pork mixed with spices, stuffed into the banana peel and boiled. As for sweets, there's the marvelous chocolate exported to the rest of the island and the world; and the popular supersweet called *cucurucho*, a coconut, ripe fruit and honey mixture served in a palm-leaf cone.

Baracoans themselves have been shaped by their environment in subtle ways. They seem perfectly in tune with the grandeur of the nature that surrounds them, accepting it with joy rather than awe and sharing it with spontaneous warmth and generosity — as they do everything else that is part of their magic reality.

SPECIALIZED TOURISM

CONVENTIONS

Convention tourism combines business with pleasure and there's no better place than Cuba to do that. So every year, artists, educators, scientists, travel agents — specialists in every imaginable field — come to Cuba where they can meet in magnificently equipped conference rooms and take field trips to a sunny beach. Cuban organizations host many of these international meetings, inviting delegates from all over the world; and associations and institutions based in other countries also select Cuba for conventions that generally include a tourist package with accommodations, some meals and sightseeing or excursions to points of interest.

Palacio de Convenciones/International Conference Center, Apartado 16046, Zona 16, La Habana, Cuba. Tel.: 21-9025. Telex: 511-609 palco cu, is Havana's main convention center, with facilities for handling several meetings simultaneously as well as exhibits and fairs in the adjacent *Pabexpo Pavilion.* A general description of the International Conference Center and its services is given in the travel section of this guide under *New Havana: On the Outskirts.*

The *Habana Libre Hotel* has two good-sized meeting-exhibit rooms and several other Havana hotels have smaller meeting rooms as do *Casa de las Américas* and many organizations and schools. At Santa María del Mar Beach east of Havana, the *Atlántico Hotel* also has meeting facilities. And many events are scheduled elsewhere on the island: for instance, Varadero, Cuba's main resort, has hosted the annual Travel Convention.

FESTIVALS

Ballet, books, crafts, films, music and theater are the main themes of the numerous festivals regularly held in Cuba. The prestigious National Ballet of Cuba sponsors a biannual *International Ballet Festival* at which Cuban and guest artists present both classics and modern ballet. Held in October-November in even-numbered years, the festival draws local and foreign ballet fans, as well as dancers, choreographers and critics.

The *New Latin-American Film Festival,* in December, is an increasingly important gathering for Latin-American film makers and critics. The festival is sponsored by the Cuban Institute of Cinematography (ICAIC) and a jury determines the winners of the coveted Coral Awards in various categories.

At the *Varadero International Music Festival*, Cuban and guest artists — mainly from Latin America and the Caribbean — play and sing the best of their popular music in a variety of styles for an enthusiastic public that fills the Varadero Amphitheater every night during this week-long spring festival.

The *Casa de las Américas Literary Awards* for the best novels, plays, and essays written in Spanish and for Portuguese and Caribbean English, French and other national language entries, are the high point of a wide range of intellectual activities sponsored by Havana's prestigious Casa de las Américas. A jury of eminent international critics and writers selects the winners in January of each year.

The *International Book Fair,* which has no fixed date, is a publishers' fair featuring books of the Spanish- and English-speaking Americas and European socialist countries. For readers of all ages, it is a great book expo.

The *Festival of Caribbean Culture,* held annually at the end of May in Santiago de Cuba, is a live demonstration of the music, dance and traditions of the Caribbean, with round-table discussions on the mixed cultures of the area.

Carnival is the most exuberant of the folk festivals regularly celebrated in Cuba (see travel section for details) and almost every city brings its own traditions to the annual festivities held at different times of the year. The best and most popular is the deeply rooted, irresistibly rhythmic Carnival of Santiago de Cuba, in July. Havana Carnival, also in July, is a more formal parade of glittering floats viewed from the grandstand, although visitors are now being encouraged to participate with costumes, floats and dances — as they do in International Carnival held at Varadero Beach during January. Sometimes, as during the *4th Havana Theater Festival* held in May-June 1987, festival activities spread all over a city. In this case, the capital's theaters, squares, parks, schools, hospitals and work places were the setting for performances by Cuban theater groups and guest actors from other Caribbean and Latin-American countries and the United States.

CUBATUR usually has an attractively priced tourist package to offer in connection with these and other festivals.

HEALTH

Cuba's advanced health care system and its pleasant climate are good reasons for visitors from abroad to look into specific medical treatment and recuperation during a tropical vacation on the island. For them, the *Cira García Central Clinic* is the place to start.

Established specifically for patients from abroad, this luxury clinic with moderate prices is directly linked to Havana's most prestigious hospitals and research labs, whose highly qualified doctors and technicians examine and treat the visiting patients. There is no limit to the range of medical services available through the Cira García, but those most frequently requested by foreigners are abortions, cosmetic surgery, complete medical examinations and weight-reducing programs, as well as two treatments invented by Cuban doctors: the repigmentation lotion *Melagenina*, only known cure for the skin disorder vitiligo; and the nearly painless needle-scissors varicose vein operation that permits the patient to walk out of the operating room and recuperate completely within a few days.

Cira García Clinic in-patients have private rooms with an extra bed for a companion, while out-patients can stay in the hotel of their choice or opt for a health vacation at Topes de Collantes, 790 m. (2600 ft.) above sea level in the Escambray Mountains. Lodgings there are in apartments, cabanas and a "kurhotel." Recovery is supervised by the medical staff of this resort-sanatorium, which has the most sophisticated diagnostic and therapeutic equipment as well as gyms, pools and other recreational facilities, including mountain climbing through wooded trails to reach breathtaking waterfalls.

For information on specific treatment, prices and tourist options, consult your travel agent or contact Health Tourism, Apartado 16046, Havana, Cuba. Tel.: 22-5511 or 22-1623. Telex: 511-609 palco cu. Facsimile: 20-2350.

The address of the Cira García Clinic is Ave. 20 e/ Ave. 41 y 19-A, Miramar, Havana, Cuba. Tel.: 2-6811 to 14 and 2-4493.

SPORTS

Bird Watching

Cuba's wooded national parks are the main refuge for some 380 species of birds, 21 of them endemic, that inhabit the island. Bird watchers from northern countries are entranced by the variety of winged creatures they have spotted on field trips. These bird-watching tours are organized with an expert leader who knows the terrain and the species. The best birding region on the island is the Zapata Peninsula (see travel section, under Matanzas Province), but Soroa and La Güira National Park in Pinar del Río (see travel section) are also admired by those who hunt with binoculars.

Fishing

In the Gulf Stream waters off the north coast of Cuba, around all the offshore cays and islets and in the hundreds of artificial and natural inland lakes, fish of all kinds abound: marlin, bonefish, wahoo, barracuda, sawfish, tuna, red snapper, jurel, permit and many others lure deep-sea fishermen, while the sportive largemouth bass is the most prized freshwater species.

The traditional *Ernest Hemingway Marlin Fishing Tournament* is held in late May, when dozens of boats set out from the Hemingway Marina west of Havana. Fishermen come from all parts of the world to participate in this exciting and usually rewarding competition for the white marlin that run in the Gulf Stream at this time of year. In August, the season for blue marlin, a second tourney is held. Both follow the regulations of the International Game Fish Association and awards are made for individual and team records.

Most of the other saltwater fish mentioned are found off the coast of Havana, Varadero and Cienfuegos. Bonefish are especially abundant around the Jardines de la Reina Archipelago off the southern coast of Ciego de Avila Province and tarpon is plentiful there as well as all along the northern coast.

Fishing boats and tackle can be rented at all seaside resorts.

Largemouth bass, brought to Cuba from the southern lakes of the United States in 1928, were quickly propagated throughout the island and can now be caught in most of Cuba's lakes. The largest bass have been caught at Lake Hanabanilla, in the Escambray Mountains of Villa Clara Province; Lake Cuyaguateje in Pinar del Río; La Redonda, in Ciego de Avila; and Zaza, in Sancti Spíritus.

Hunting

The entire archipelago of Cuba falls within the corridor for migratory birds that fly south in winter and join the many permanent cynegetic residents on the largest island in the Antilles. These birds are supported by an aquatic infrastructure that includes hundreds of lakes, ponds, rivers and streams, 120 recently built reservoirs and 453 kilometers of canals.

The island's main hunting reserves are Maspotón, in Pinar del Río; Morón and Aguachales de Falla, in Ciego de Avila; the Isle of Youth; Varadero; the recently opened

Cerro de Caisimú, in Las Tunas; and Los Caneyes de Virama, in Granma. Hunters usually come in groups and their travel agents make prior arrangements with CUBATUR for hunting licenses and accommodations at a reserve, where gear can also be rented. The hunting season varies according to species: white-crowned pigeons, July-October; mourning and white-winged doves, September-February; fulvous tree ducks, September-March; other ducks, American coots, common snipes, common guinea fowl and pheasants, October-March. Some reserves also have wild pigs and wild boar.

Scuba diving

Cuba's 400 km. (260 mi.) of offshore coral reefs are the main attraction for scuba divers, who can view breathtaking underwater landscapes almost anywhere around the island. The famous Pirates' Coast on the Isle of Youth (where the International Scuba Diving Headquarters are located); the East Havana beaches; Varadero; Santa Lucía in Camagüey; and Guardalavaca in Holguín all have sites marked for their great beauty and interest. Scuba-diving groups generally favor the Isle of Youth, but individual tourists are also welcome there and at all the other resorts listed in the travel section as offering dives.

STUDY

Foreign students, scientists, professionals and teachers have an opportunity to enroll in courses and conference cycles programmed by Cuba's Ministries of Education and Higher Education in cooperation with CUBATUR.

Folkcuba, a two-week workshop in percussion and dance offered by the National Folklore Group in late January and early July, covers rumba, conga, bantu and yoruba rhythms for beginninners and advanced students at $150 to $250, depending on level. Lodgings (double occupancy) and meals cost another $300.

Intensive Spanish language courses designed for both

beginning and advanced foreign students are offered at the Universities of Havana and Matanzas. Limited to a minimum of 10 and a maximum of 30 students, these month-long courses have 80 class hours (four hours a day Monday through Friday). Registration is $100 USD for the beginning course and $150 for the advanced. The CUBATUR tourist package provides accommodations in a class A hotel in Havana or a class B hotel in Varadero, double occupancy MAP (breakfast and dinner).

The University of Havana and the Central University of Villa Clara have postgraduate conference cycles in agricultural sciences, animal sciences, arts and letters, economics and law, electronics and engineering, mathematics and other fields. The conferences are given in Spanish for a minimum of 10 and a maximum of 30 students and cover 20 lecture hours (four hours a day Monday through Friday). The enrollment fee is $50 USD. On the Havana circuit, the eight-day tourist program includes lodgings, airport-hotel-airport transfers, briefing session and welcome cocktails, transportation to all programmed activities and a tour of Old Havana. On the Villa Clara circuit, the 11-day program includes lodgings, airport-hotel-airport transfers, briefing session and welcome cocktails, a tour of Old Havana and a visit to the Guamá tourist center in Matanzas Province.

University of Havana

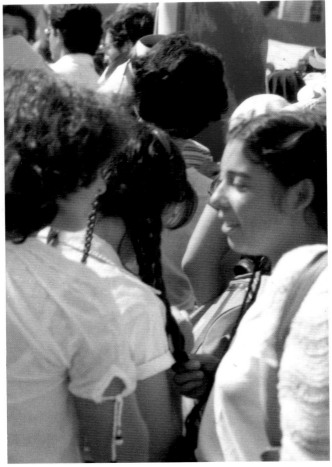

Latin-American students wait to march in May Day parade

GETTING TO KNOW CUBA IN SPANISH

These miniconversations will help you communicate with Cubans in day-to-day situations. Just read the phonetic spellings using standard English sounds (pronouncing "a" as in father and "e" as in better unless otherwise indicated).

In general, Cubans give vowels a staccato articulation and soften consonants, even to the point of swallowing those in unaccented syllables (accented syllables are underlined). The "r" and "rr" are difficult sounds for English-speaking people but can be approximated by pressing the tip of the tongue against the teeth.

Note that most Spanish nouns ending in "o" are masculine and take the article "el," while most ending in "a" are feminine and take the article "la": **el niño / la niña** (el neen-yo / la neen-ya), meaning the baby (boy / girl). Adjectives agree in gender with nouns: **la escuela nueva / el carro viejo** (la es-kwe-la nwe-va / el ka-rro vee-e-ho), meaning the new school / the old car.

TEN MINICONVERSATIONS

1. Greetings and Introductions

Good morning (good afternoon, good evening).
Buenos días (buenas tardes, buenas noches).
Bwe-nos dee-as (bwe-nas tar-des, bwe-nas no-ches).

What's your name?
¿Cómo se llama usted?
Ko-mo say ya-ma oos-ted?

My name is _____ .
Me llamo _____ .
May ya-mo _____ .

Do you speak English? Yes. No.
¿Habla usted inglés? Sí. No.
A-bla oos-ted een-gles? See. No.

I don't understand. Please talk more slowly (repeat it, write it down).
No entiendo. Favor de hablar más despacio (repetir, escribirlo).
No en-tee-en-do. Fa-vor de a-blar mas des-pa-cio (re-pe-teer, es-kree-beer-lo).

Thank you. You're welcome.
Gracias. De nada.
Gra-cias. De na-da.

I would like to introduce my wife (husband, daughter, son, friend).
Quiero presentar a mi esposa (marido, hija, hijo, amigo [a].
Kee-e-ro pre-sen-tar a mee es-po-sa (ma-ree-do, ee-ha, ee-ho, a-mee-go [a].

Pleased to meet you. Delighted.
Mucho gusto. Encantado [a].
Mu-cho gus-to. En-kan-ta-do [a].

I must go now. See you later (soon, tomorrow). Good-bye.
Ahora tengo que irme. Hasta luego (pronto, mañana). Adiós.
A-o-ra ten-go kay eer-me. As-ta lwe-go (pron-to, man-ya-na). A-dee-os.

2. Money and Shopping

Can you cash this traveler's check for me?
¿Puede cambiarme este cheque de viajero?
Pwe-de kam-bee-ar-may es-te che-ke de vee-a-he-ro?

Where can I buy rum (cigars, souvenirs, clothing, toiletries, records, posters, books)?
¿Dónde puedo comprar ron (tabacos, suvenirs, ropa, artículos de tocador, discos, afiches, libros)?

Don-de pwe-do kom-prar ron (ta-ba-kos, su-ve-neers, ropa, ar-tee-ku-los de to-ka-dor, dees-kos, a-fee-ches, lee-
bros)?

Do you have a larger (smaller) size?
¿Tiene una talla más grande (chiquita)?
Tee-en-e oo-na ta-ya mas gran-de (chee-kee-ta)?

It's very cheap. It's too expensive.
Está muy barato. Está demasiado caro.
Es-ta mu-ee ba-ra-to. Es-ta de-ma-see-a-do ka-ro.

I'll take this please. That's all, thank you.
Quiero esto, por favor. Nada más, gracias.
Kee-e-ro es-to, por fa-vor. Na-da mas gra-cias.

Where's the cashier? I'm waiting for my change.
¿Dónde está el cajero? Estoy esperando el vuelto.
Don-de es-ta el ka-he-ro? Es-toy es-pe-ran-do el vwel-to.

3. Catching the Bus

Please tell me what bus goes to Old Havana? Arms Square?
¿Por favor, qué guagua me lleva a la Habana Vieja? ¿A la Plaza de Armas?
Por fa-vor kay wa-wa may ye-va a la a-ba-na vee-e-ha? A la pla-sa de ar-mas?

Where is the bus stop?
¿Dónde está la parada de la guagua?
Don-de es-ta la pa-ra-da de la wa-wa?

Walk one (two, three) block(s) to the left (right, straight ahead).
Camine una (dos, tres) cuadra(s) a la izquierda (la derecha, recta).
Ka-mee-ne oo/-na (dos, tres) kwa-dras a la ees-key-er-da (de-re-cha, rec-ta).

I need some nickels.
Me hace falta unos medios.
May a-se fal-ta oo-nos may-dee-os.

Should I get off here or at the next stop?
¿Me quedo aquí o en la próxima parada?
May <u>kay</u>-do a-<u>kee</u> o en la <u>prok</u>-see-ma pa-<u>ra</u>-da?

4. Driving

Give me 20 liters of gas.
Echeme veinte litros de gasolina.
<u>Ay</u>-che-me <u>vayn</u>-te <u>lee</u>-tros de gas-o-<u>leen</u>-a.

Please check the oil (water, brake fluid, air).
Favor de revisar el aceite (agua, líquido de frenos, aire).
Fa-<u>vor</u> de re-vee-<u>sar</u> el a-<u>se</u>-te (a-gwa, <u>lee</u>-kee-do de <u>fray</u>-nos, <u>I</u>-re).

I had a flat. Can you fix the tire?
Se me ponchó. ¿Puede reparar la goma?
Say may pon-<u>cho</u>. <u>Pwe</u>-de re-pa-<u>rar</u> la <u>go</u>-ma?

The car won't start. What's wrong? The battery needs charging.
No arranca el carro. ¿Qué tiene? Hay que cargar el acumulador.
<u>No</u> a-<u>rran</u>-ka el <u>ca</u>-rro. <u>Kay</u> tee-<u>en</u>-e? <u>I</u> kay kar-<u>gar</u> el a-ku-mu-la-<u>dor</u>.

Which way to . . . . ?
¿El camino hacia. . . . ?
El ka-<u>mee</u>-no a-<u>see</u>-a . . . ?

5. Taking Pictures

May I take some pictures here?
¿Puedo tirar algunas fotos aquí?
<u>Pwe</u>-do tee-<u>rar</u> al-<u>goon</u>-as <u>fo</u>-tos a-<u>kee</u>?

May I take your picture?
¿Me permite retratarle?
May per-<u>mee</u>-te re-tra-<u>tar</u>-le?

Move closer. Hold it!
Acérquense. ¡No se muevan!
A-<u>ser</u>-ken-se. No say <u>mwe</u>-van!

Look here and smile. Don't look at the camera.
Miren acá con sonrisa. No miren a la cámara.
Mee-ren a-ka kon son-ree-sa. No mee-ren a la ka-ma-ra.

Wait a minute. One more, please. That's great!
Espere un momento. Una más, por favor. ¡Magnífico!
Es-pe-re oon mo-men-to. Oon-a mas, por fa-vor. Mag-neef-ee-ko!

No photos allowed.
Prohibidas las fotos.
Pro-ee-bee-das las fo-tos.

6. Problems

Can you help me, **compañero**? I'm lost.
¿Compañero [a], me puede ayudar? Estoy extraviado [a].
Kom-pan-ye-ro [a], me pwe-de a-yu-dar? Es-toy es-tra-vee-a-do [a].

I'm looking for my friends (my hotel, this address).
Busco a mis amigos (mi hotel, esta dirección).
Boos-ko a mees a-mee-gos (mee o-tel, es-ta dee-rec-see-on.

I've lost my purse (wallet, key, passport).
Perdí mi cartera (monedero, llave, pasaporte).
Per-dee mee kar-te-ra (mo-ne-de-ro, ya-ve, pas-a-por-te).

Look out! What's going on? Go away!
¡Cuidado! ¿Qué pasa? ¡Váyase!
Kwee-da-do! Kay pa-sa? Va-ya-se!

Please solve this problem.
Favor de arreglar este inconveniente.
Fa-vor de a-rre-glar es-te een-kon-ven-yen-te.

7. Sports and Recreation

Let's go to the beach.
Vamos a la playa.
Va-mos a la pla-ya.

Where can we swim (scuba dive, fish, rent a boat)?
¿Dónde podemos nadar (bucear, pescar, alquilar botes)?

Don-de po-de-mos na-dar, boo-say-ar, pes-kar, al-kee-lar bo-tes)?

I like to run (ride horseback, go bicycling).
Me gusta correr (montar a caballo, ir en bicicleta).
Me goos-ta ko-rrer (mon-tar-a ka-ba-yo, eer en bee-see-kle-ta).

8. In Case of Illness

I feel ill (better).
Me siento mal (mejor).
May see-en-to mal (me-hor).

I feel faint. She (he) fainted.
Tengo fatiga. Se desmayó.
Ten-go fa-tee-ga. Say des-ma-yo.

I have a headache (a stomach ache, diarrhea).
Tengo dolor de cabeza (dolor de estómago, diarrea).
Ten-go do-lor de ka-bay-sa (do-lor de es-to-ma-go, dee-a-ree-a).

This tooth hurts. I do not want it pulled.
Me duele este diente. No quiero que me lo saque.
May dwe-le es-te dee-en-te. No key-e-ro kay may lo sa-ke.

Please take me to the polyclinic (hospital).
Favor de llevarme al policlínico (hospital).
Fa-vor de ye-var-me al po-lee-kleen-ee-ko (os-pee-tal).

Where can I buy medicine? Is there a pharmacy nearby?
¿Dónde puedo comprar medicina? ¿Hay una farmacia cerca?
Don-de pwe-do kom-prar me-dee-see-na? I oon-a far-ma-see-a ser-ka?

9. Night Life

I'd like to go to the ballet (the theater, a concert, an art exhibit, a cabaret.)
Quisiera ir al ballet (al teatro, a un concierto, a una galería de arte, a un cabaret).

Kee-see-er-a eer al ba-le (al te-a-tro, a oon kon-see-er-to, a oon-a gal-er-ee-a de ar-te, a oon ka-ba-re.

What time does the performance start? Can you get tickets for me?

¿A qué hora empieza la función? ¿Me puede conseguir la entrada?

A kay o-ra em-pee-e-sa la foon-see-on? May pwe-de kon-se-geer la en-tra-da?

Cuban music is very rhythmic. Show me how to dance the *son* (rumba, cha-cha, conga).

La música cubana es muy rítmica. Enséñeme a bailar el son (rumba, cha-cha-cha, conga).

La mu-see-ka cu-ba-na es mu-ee reet-mee-ka. En-sen-ye-me a by-lar el son, (room-ba, cha-cha-cha, kon-ga).

10. Wining and Dining

I would like to reserve a table for four for dinner (lunch) at:

Quisiera reservar una mesa para cuatro personas para la comida (el almuerzo) en:

Kee-see-e-ra re-ser-var oon-a may-sa pa-ra kwa-tro per-son-as pa-ra la ko-mee-da (el al-mwer-so) en:

Please show us the menu. We're ready to order.

La carta, por favor. Queremos pedir.

La kar-ta por fa-vor. Ke-re-mos pe-deer.

Please bring us water (cocktails, beer, red wine, white wine, a fork, a knife, a spoon, a napkin).

Favor de traernos agua (cocteles, cerveza, vino tinto, vino blanco, un tenedor, un cuchillo, una cuchara, una servi-lleta).

Fa-vor de tra-er-nos a-gwa (kok-tel-es, ser-ve-sa, vee-no teen-to, vee-no blan-ko, oon te-ne-dor, oon koo-chee-yo, oon-a koo-cha-ra, oon-a ser-vee-ye-ta).

The check, please.

La cuenta, por favor.

la kwayn-ta por fa-vor.

EATING VOCABULARY

Now look for the following listings on the menu:

aguacate / a-gwa-ka-te — avocado
ajiaco / a-hee-a-ko — meat and vegetable stew
arroz / a-rros — rice
asado / a-sa-do — roast
biftec / beef-tek — beef steak
bocadito / bo-ka-dee-to —sandwich
camarones / ca-ma-ron-es — shrimp
cerdo / ser-do — pork
conejo / con-ay-ho — rabbit
cordero / kor-de-ro — lamb
cherna / cher-na — giant bass
chicharrón / chee-cha-rron — cracklings
chorizo / cho-ree-so — pork sausage
chuleta / chu-le-ta — chop
ensalada / en-sa-la-da — salad
filete / fee-let-e — filet
flan / flan — custard
frijoles / free-ho-les — dried beans
frito / free-to — fried
frutas / frut-as — fruit
guayaba / gwa-ya-ba — guava
habichuelas / a-bee-chwe-las — string beans
hamburguesa / am-boor-gay-sa — hamburger
helado / e-la-do — ice cream
huevos / way-vos — eggs
jamón / ha-mon — ham
langosta / lan-gos-ta — lobster
langostino / lan-gos-teen-o — prawn
lechón / le-chon — suckling pig
lomo / lo-mo — loin
mantequilla / man-te-kee-ya — butter
mariscos / ma-rees-kos — shellfish
naranja / na-ran-ha — orange
oca / oh-ka — goose
ostiones / os-tee-on-es — oysters

pan / pan — bread
pargo / par-go — red snapper
pavo / pa-vo — turkey
pescado / pes-ka-do — fish
picadillo / pee-ka-dee-yo — chopped beef
piña / peen-ya — pineapple
plátanos / pla-ta-nos — bananas
pollo / po-yo — chicken
queso / kay-so — cheese
salsa / sal-sa — sauce
ternera / ter-ner-a — veal
toronja / to-ron-ha — grapefruit
tortilla / tor-tee-ya — omelet
tostada / tos-ta-da — toast
tostones / tos-ton-es — fried plantains
vegetales / ve-he-tal-es — vegetables
yogur / yo-goor — yogurt

GLOSSARY OF USEFUL WORDS AND PHRASES

Days of the Week
(**los días de la semana** / los dee-as de la se-ma-na)

Sunday	**domingo**	do-meen-go
Monday	**lunes**	loo-nes
Tuesday	**martes**	mar-tes
Wednesday	**miércoles**	mee-er-ko-les
Thursday	**jueves**	hwe-ves
Friday	**viernes**	vee-er-nes
Saturday	**sábado**	sa-ba-do

Today, yesterday, tomorrow. **Hoy, ayer, mañana.** Oy, a-yer, man-ya-na.

Months of the Year
(**los meses del año** / los me-ses del an-yo)

January	**enero**	e-ne-ro
February	**febrero**	fe-bre-ro
March	**marzo**	mar-so

April	**abril**	a-breel
May	**mayo**	ma-yo
June	**junio**	hoon-ee-o
July	**julio**	hool-ee-o
August	**agosto**	a-gos-to
September	**septiembre**	se-tee-em-bre
October	**octubre**	oc-tu-bre
November	**noviembre**	no-vee-em-bre
December	**diciembre**	dee-see-em-bre

This year, last year, next year. **Este año, el año pasado, el próximo año.** Es-te an-yo, el an-yo pa-sa-do, el pro-si-mo an-yo.

Time, Distance, Numbers
(el tiempo, la distancia, los números
el tee-em-po, la dees-tan-ceea, los num-e-ros)

What time is it? **¿Qué hora es?** Kay o-ra es?
It's 1, 2:30, 9:45. **Es la una; son las dos y media, las diez menos quince.** Es la oon-a; son las dos ee may-dee-a, las dee-es me-nos keen-se.

When? How long? How far?
¿Cuándo? ¿Cuánto tiempo? ¿A qué distancia?
Kwan-do? Kwan-to tee-em-po? A kay dees-tan-ceea?

1	oon-o [a]	15	keen-se
2	dos	16	dee-es-e-says
3	trays	17	dee-es-e-see-e-te
4	kwa-tro	18	dee-es-e-o-cho
5	seen-ko	19	dee-es-e-nwe-ve
6	se-ees	20	vayn-te
7	see-e-te	30	trayn-te
8	o-cho	40	kwar-en-ta
9	nwe-ve	50	seen-cwen-ta
10	dee-es	60	se-sen-ta
11	on-se	70	se-ten-ta
12	do-se	80	o-chen-ta
13	tray-se	90	no-ven-ta
14	ka-tor-se	100	see-en

In the Hotel

(**en el hotel** / en el o-<u>tel</u>)

I have a room reservation for tonight.
Tengo una habitación reservada para la noche de hoy.
<u>Ten</u>-go <u>oon</u>-a a-bee-ta-see-<u>on</u> re-ser-<u>va</u>-da pa-ra la <u>no</u>-che de <u>oy</u>.

Your room is on the second floor. Here is the key. Where is your luggage?
Su habitación está en el segundo piso. Esta es la llave. ¿Dónde está su equipaje?
Su a-bee-ta-see-<u>on</u> es-<u>ta</u> en el se-<u>goon</u>-do <u>pee</u>-so. <u>Es</u>-ta es la <u>ya</u>-ve. <u>Don</u>-de es-<u>ta</u> su e-kee-pa-<u>he</u>?

Please show your guest card when requesting hotel services.
Favor de mostrar su tarjeta de huésped para pedir los servicios del hotel.
Fa-<u>vor</u> de mo-<u>strar</u> su tar-<u>he</u>-ta de <u>wes</u>-ped pa-ra pe-<u>deer</u> los ser-<u>vee</u>-cios del ho-<u>tel</u>.

Guests should pay their bills at the front desk.
Los huéspedes deben pagar sus cuentas en la carpeta.
Los <u>wes</u>-pe-des <u>day</u>-ben pa-<u>gar</u> sus <u>kwayn</u>-tas en la kar-<u>pet</u>-a.

Wake me at. . . .
Despiérteme a las. . . .
Des-<u>pier</u>-te-may a las. . . .

I'm in a hurry.
Estoy apurado [a].
Es-<u>toy</u> a-poo-<u>ra</u>-do [a].

I think there's a mistake.
Creo que hay una equivocación.
<u>Kray</u>-o kay I <u>oon</u>-a e-kee-vo-ka-see-<u>on</u>.

May I speak to the manager?
¿Puedo hablar con el administrador?
<u>Pwe</u>-do a-<u>blar</u> kon el ad-mee-nee-stra-<u>dor</u>?

Please bring me . . .
Me quiere traer. . . .
May kee-e-re tra-er. . . .

— a towel	**una toalla**	oon-a to-a-ya
— soap	**jabón**	ha-bon
— toilet paper	**papel sanitario**	pa-pel sa-nee-ta-ree-o
— a light bulb	**un bombillo**	oon bom-bee-yo
— hangers	**percheros**	per-che-ros
— drinking water	**agua potable**	a-gwa po-tab-le
— a glass	**un vaso**	oon vas-o
— a bottle opener	**un abridor**	oon a-bree-dor

The bathroom (wash basin, tub, shower, toilet). . . .
El baño (el lavamanos, la bañadera, la ducha, el servicio sanitario). . . .
El ban-yo (el la-va-man-os, la ban-ya-day-ra, la doo-cha, el ser-vee-ceeo san-ee-ta-ree-o. . . .

— is dirty	**está sucio [a]**	es-ta su-cio [a]
— is broken	**está roto [a]**	es-ta ro-to [a]
— is stopped up	**está tupido [a]**	es-ta tu-pee-do [a]
— doesn't work	**no funciona**	no foon-see-on-a

How long will the laundry take? Please press this.
¿Cuánto tardará la lavandería? Favor de planchar esto.
Kwan-to tar-da-ra la la-van-de-ree-a? Fa-vor de plan-char es-to.

This is not mine.
Esto no es mío.
Es-to no es mee-o.

Room service.
Servicio de habitación.
Ser-vee-cio de a-bee-ta-see-on.

You can make up the room now.
Puede hacer la habitación ahora.
Pwe-de a-ser la ha-bee-ta-see-on a-o-ra.

Come in. Come later.
Entre. Venga más tarde.
En-tre. Ven-ga mas tar-de.

Excuse me. Of course.
Discúlpeme. No importa.
Dee-skool-pe-may. No im-por-ta.

hot/cold	**caliente/frío [a]**	kal-ee-en-te / free-o [a]
up/down	**arriba/abajo**	a-rree-ba / a-ba-ho
open/closed	**abierto [a]/ cerrado [a]**	a-bee-er-to [a] / ce-rra-do [a]
good/bad	**bueno [a]/malo [a]**	bwe-no [a] / mal-o [a]
old/new/young	**viejo [a]/nuevo [a]/ joven**	vee-ay-ho [a] / nwe-vo [a] / ho-ven

Telephone Calls

(llamadas telefónicas / ya-ma-das te-le-fon-ee-kas)

Operator, I want to make a long-distance call.
Operadora, quiero poner una llamada de larga distancia.
O-pe-ra-do-ra, key-e-ro po-ner oon-a ya-ma-da de lar-ga dees-tan-cia.

I want to speak to. . . .
Quiero hablar con. . . .
Key-e-ro a-blar kon . . .

I was cut off.
Me cortaron la linea.
May kor-ta-ron la leen-ea.

It's the wrong number.
Número equivocado.
Noo-me-ro e-kee-vo-ka-do.

Hold the line.
No cuelgue.
No kuel-gay.

The line is busy.
Está ocupada.
Es-ta o-ku-pa-da.

There's no answer.
No responden / contestan.
No res-pon-den / kon-tes-tan.

INDEX

Abarca, Silvestre, 67
Abra Campsite, 84-85
Abra Farm, 94
Abreu, Don Pedro, 111
Abreu de Estévez, María, 111
Academy of Sciences, 66
Africa House, 54-55
Afro-Cuban culture, 19, 55, 69,
    75, 76, 82, 112, 151, 159. *See
    also* Carnival
Agramonte, Ignacio, 130-131, 133
Agrarian Reform Law, 35
Aguachales de Falla, 128, 171
airlines, 2, 45; domestic, 13-14,
    15
airplanes, private, 2-3
Albear, Francisco de, 63
Aldama Palace, 65
Alejandro García Caturla Music
    Museum, 112
Alexander von Humboldt
    Museum of Natural Sciences,
    123
Alvarez López, Pelayo, 166
Ambos Mundos Hotel, 54
Américas mansion, 100-102
Anaquillé Theater Group, 52
Ancón Beach, 125
Angel Hill, 61
animals. *See* flora and fauna
Aponte, José Antonio, 22
aquariums, 77, 161
Arabe Restaurant, 83
Archaeological Mural, 90-91
Archaeological Valley, 160
armed forces, 37
Armored Train Monument, 110
Arms Museum, 51
Arms Square, 47-55, 48
arts and crafts, 55, 57, 60, 96,
    108-109, 149, 166
Ascunce Domenech, Manuel,
    110

Atlántico Hotel, 84, 167
Automobile Museum, 52
automobiles, 52; for rent, 12-13

Bacardí Moreau, Emilio, 152
Baconao Park, 10, 159-161
Bacuranao Beach, 83
Bahía de Miel (Bay of Honey),
    163-164
Bailén Beach, 92
ballet, 42, 66, 131, 167-168
Balneario del Sol, 160
Banes, 138
Baracoa, 18, 162-166
Bariay Beach, 138
Bariay National Park, 137
baseball, 40-41
Batista, Fulgencio, 32, 34, 60, 93
Bay of Pigs, 36, 109
Bayamo, 18, 24, 140-142
Bayona, Count de, 57
beaches, 9-10, 92, 97, 98-103,
    120, 128, 132, 137, 138, 143-45,
    161, 163; East Havana, 83-85,
    172
Bellamar Cave, 106
Benito Juárez Cuba-Mexico
    Friendship House, 54
Betancourt, Ana, 133-134
Bibijagua Beach, 96
bird watching, 10-11, 88, 109, 170
blacks in Cuba, 19, 22, 30, 35,
    42. *See also* Afro-Cuban
    culture; slavery
Blue Circuit, 83-84
Bobadilla, Doña Inés de, 50
Bodeguita del Medio Restaurant,
    59-60
bookstores, 63, 64-65
botanical gardens, 10, 81, 86, 87,
    120, 161
Brunet Palace, 123
buses, 15, 74; local (*guaguas*), 12

Cabaña Fortress, 50, 67-68
cabarets, 14-15
Cabildo Teatral, 150
Cabrales, María, 26
Caibarién, 115-116
Calixto García Revolution
    Square, 136
Calixto García Park, 134-135
Camacho, Tomás, 87
Camagüey, 18, 129-132
Camagüey Province, 129-134
Camilo Cienfuegos Sugarmill, 68
Camp Columbia, 34
campsites, 15, 16, 84-85, 86-87,
    89, 115, 160
Canada, tourism from, 1, 2, 3,
    7, 132, 137, 144-145
Canarreos Archipelago, 97
Canchánchara, 124
Caneyes, 109-111
carabalí street dances, 18, 19, 45,
    151-152
Cárdenas, 98, 106-107
Caridad Theater, 110
Carlos de la Torre Museum of
    Natural History, 135
Carnival, 41, 103, 168-169; in
    Havana, 41, 70, 168-169; in
    Santiago de Cuba, 41, 151-
    152, 168
Carnival Museum, 150
Cartelera, 43
Casablanca, 68-69
Casa de las Américas, 76, 167
Casa de las Américas Literary
    Awards, 168
Casa de las Infusiones, 54
Casona Restaurant, 89
Castillo (in Baracoa), 163-164
Castillo de las Nubes, 87
Castro Ruz, Fidel, 32-34, 36, 37,
    38, 54-55, 61, 82, 94
Castro, Raúl, 33, 37, 38
Cathedral of Havana, 56, 58-59
Cathedral of San Carlos, 106

Cathedral Square, 56-60
Catholic Church, 21, 58, 159. See
    also individual churches
Caturla, Alejandro García, 112
Cayo Coco, 128
Cayo Conuco, 115
Cayo Fragosa, 116
Cayo Granma, 155
Cayo Guillermo, 128-129
Cayo Largo, 13, 97
Cayo Levisa, 91
Cecilia Restaurant, 77
Cecilia Valdés, 59, 61, 62
Central University of Villa
    Clara, 110, 173
ceramics, 96, 108-109
Céspedes, Carlos Manuel de,
    23, 49, 133, 140-142, 148, 153
Céspedes Park, 148-149
Cepero y Nieto, Doña María de,
    49-50
China, immigration from, 22-23
Ciboney Indians, 17
Ciego de Avila, 127
Ciego de Avila Province, 127-129
Ciego Montero Spring, 120
Cienfuegos, 171
Cienfuegos, José, 118
Cienfuegos Naval Base, 120
Cienfuegos Province, 118-120
Cigar Salon, 53
cigars, Cuban 53, 90, 92
Cira García Central Clinic, 169-
    170
clothing, recommended, 4
Clouet, Louis de, 118
Cobre, 156
Coloradas Beach, 143-144
Colored Independence Party, 30
Columbus, Christopher, 17, 50,
    59, 93, 137, 138, 162, 165
Committees for the Defense of
    the Revolution (CDR), 37
Communist Party of Cuba
    (PCC), 38, 75

Constitution, 38; of 1901, 29-30
consulates in Cuba, 5-7
conventions, 78, 167
Coral prizes, 42
Cortés, Hernando, 18, 123
Crane, Hart, 94-95
Crane, Stephen, 29
credit cards, 5
Cross of Parra, 165-166
Cuban Institute of Cinematography (ICAIC), 42, 73
Cuban Revolutionary Party, 27-28
CUBATUR, 9, 15, 169, 172-173
Cuchillas de Baracoa Mountains, 163
Cueva Tavern, 57
currency, 4-5, 16
customs regulations, 3
Cuyaguateje lake, 92

Daiquiri, 63
Day of National Liberation (January 1), 4
Day of National Rebellion (July 26), 4
Demajagua, 23, 140, 142-143
de Soto, Hernando, 50, 51
Dominica Hotel, 106-107
Dos Ríos, 156
Duaba, 28
Duaba Beach, 163
Du Pont, Irénée, 98-99, 100, 101

East Havana beaches, 83-852
Echeverría, José Antonio, 107
education, 40, 59, 111. *See also* universities
Education Museum, 57
electric current, 4
Elguea Baths, 116
Emilio Bacardí Museum, 152
Ernest Hemingway Marlin Fishing Tournament, 79, 82, 171

Escalera, 22
Escaleras de Jaruco Park, 82
Escambray Mountains, 10, 40, 43, 116, 121, 124, 170
Escambray Theater Group, 42
Esperanza, 91
Espín, Vilma, 33-34
Espíritu Santo Church, 55-56
Experimental Graphics Workshop, 57

fashion houses, 76-77
Federation of Cuban Women, 37, 75
Felipe Poey Museum of Natural Sciences, 66
Festival of Caribbean Culture, 168
Figueredo, Pedro, 24
Figueredo, "Perucho", 140-141
films, 42-43, 73, 168
fishing, 79, 82, 88, 92, 103, 117, 126, 127-128, 129, 170-171
flora and fauna, 10-11, 51-52, 87, 107, 108, 115, 135, 163, 166. *See also* botanical gardens; fishing; hunting; wildlife preserves
Florida, 132
Floridita Restaurant, 53, 54
Fondo de Bienes Culturales (Foundation for Cultural Assets), 55
Fort Matachín, 163, 164
Fountain of Youth, 76
Fraternity Park, 65

Gaggini, Giuseppe, 50, 56, 65
García, Gen. Calixto, 26, 29, 76, 134, 135, 136, 159
García Lorca (Great Theater of Havana), 66
Gibara, 138
Giménez, Col. Don Pedro, 157
Giraldilla, 50-51

Gómez, Gen. Máximo, 28, 29, 60, 113-114
Gómez, Juan Gualberto, 28
Gómez, Panchito, 28
González, Leovigildo, 90
Grajales, Mariana, 26
Granjita Siboney, 160
Granma (boat), 33, 61, 143
Granma (newspaper), 43
Granma Province, 23, 140-145
Gran Piedra, 160
Grapefruit Festival (Isle of Youth), 93
Great Theater of Havana, 66
Greene, Graham, 63, 64
guaguas (local buses), 12
Guáimaro, 133-134
Guamá, 18, 108
Guamá Museum, 108
Guamuhaya Archaeological Museum, 123
Guanabacoa Museum, 82
Guanahacabibes Peninsula National Park, 92
Guanahatabey Indians, 17
Guantánamo (city), 162
Guantánamo Naval Base, 30, 162
Guantánamo Province, 162-166
Guardalavaca Beach, 137, 172
guayaberas, 24, 77
Guayabita del Pinar, 89
Guevara, Ernesto Che, 33, 34, 74, 89, 110
Guillén, Nicolás, 35
Güira National Park, 88-89, 170
Guiteras Holmes, Antonio, 31-32
Gulf of Guacanayabo, 142

Habaguanex, 18
Habana Libre Hotel, 70, 167
Hanabanilla Hotel, 116-117

Hatuey, 17-18
Havana, 12, 13, 45-77, 171; bookstores in, 63-64-65; Carnival in, 41, 168-169; churches in, 55-56, 58-59, 61, 64; fashion houses in, 76-77; history of, in colonial period, 19, 20, 24, 45, 48; hotels in, 52, 63, 66, 70-71, 76, 77; museums in, 49-51, 52-53, 54-55, 57-58, 60-62, 63, 64, 66, 74; music in, 60, 72, 75, 76; outskirts of, 78-85; restaurants in, 53, 54, 57, 63, 70, 71, 73, 75, 77; theaters in, 52, 66, 73, 74
Haydée Santamaría Gallery of Latin-American Art, 76
Hazard, Samuel, 52
health care, 16, 39-40, 70, 111, 145, 169-170
health regulations for visitors, 3
health tourism, 121, 169-70. *See also* mineral waters
Hemingway, Ernest, 79, 82; places frequented by, 53, 54, 63, 79, 82, 79
Hemingway Marina, 79
Hemingway Museum, 82
Heredia, José María, 150
Hernández, Melba, 33
Hershey Sugarmill, 68
Hicacos Peninsula. *See also* Varadero Beach, 98
History Will Absolve Me, 33
Holguín, 13, 45, 134-137
Holguín Province, 134-139
holidays, 4
hotels, 15, 16. House of Comedy, 52
Hoyos, Juan and Rodrigo de, 156, 157
hunting, 11, 88, 96, 126, 127, 128, 171-172; seasons for, 172

Iñiguez Landín, Lucía, 136
Indian Cave, 90
Indian Maiden Fountain (Noble
    Havana), 65
Indians, pre-Columbian, 48, 98,
    109-110, 123; artifacts of, 73,
    95-96, 108, 135, 138-139, 146,
    164; Spanish conquerors and,
    17-18, 130
Internacional Hotel, 99, 102, 103
International Book Fair, 168
International Conference
    Center, 78, 167
International Music Festival, 103
INTUR, 76
investments, US, 26-27, 31
Isabelica Museum, 160
Islands in the Stream, 63
Isle of Pines, 25, 30, 33, 94. *See
    also* Isle of Youth
Isle of Youth, 13, 14, 92-96, 171,
    172

Jagua Castle, 119
Jardines de la Reina Archipelago,
    171
Jibacoa Beach, 83, 84
Jigüe, 34, 145
José Antonio Echeverría
    Museum, 107
José Martí Museum, 64
José Martí Pioneer City, 84
José Martí Theater, 65
July 26, 4
Junco Palace, 105

Lake Hanabanilla, 116-117
Lake Zaza, 126
land reform, 35
Las Casas, Bartolomé de, 18,
    124
Last Paradise, 129
Leche Lagoon, 127-128
Lenin Hill, 69

Lenin Park, 80-81
literacy, 35; campaign of 1961
    for, 57, 110
Lombillo mansion, 57
Longo, Rita, 72, 108
López, Narciso, 106
Louvre sidewalk, 66

Maceo, Gen. Antonio, 66
Maceo Park, 70
Maceo y Grajales, Gen.
    Antonio, 26, 28, 70, 153, 163
Machado, Gerardo, 31, 73
machismo, 37, 44
Maguana Beach, 163
Maine, 28-29, 71
Malecón (in Havana), 69-70, 76
Mambí liberation fighters, 24,
    29, 124, 159
Manacas-Iznagas Tower, 125
Manicaragua, 116
Manuel Ascunce Domenech
    Teachers' Training School, 110
Manzanillo, 13, 142
maps, 13
Marazul Tours, 1
Marea del Portillo Beach, 144-
    145
Marriage Palace, 66
Martí, José, 24-25, 26, 27-28, 30,
    62, 94, 153, 156; commemora-
    tion of, 57, 62, 64, 66, 75, 112,
    153, 156
Martínez, Fray Jacinto María, 62
Martínez, José, 139
Martínez Sopena, Sergio, 73
Martí Park, 112
Mascotte Hotel, 113
Maspotón, 88, 171
Matachín Municipal Museum,
    164
Matanzas, 68, 104-106
Matanzas Province, 98-109
May 1 Boarding School, 110

Maya, 30
Mayabe Lookout, 136
May Day, 4
Media Luna, 143
Mella, Julio Antonio, 31, 73
Mendive, Rafael María, 24-25
Menéndez, Jesús, 142
Mesón de la Flota, 52
Milanés, José Jacinto, 106
mineral waters, 88, 91, 116, 120
Ministry of Communications, 74
Ministry of Education, 54
Ministry of the Interior, 74
miracles, 156-157
Miramar neighborhood
    (Havana), 13, 76
Modern Dance Company, 42
Moncada Garrison, 4, 32, 146,
    148, 160
Montané Anthropological
    Museum, 73
Monte Piedad, 52-53
Mora, Ignacio, 133-134
Morgan, Henry, 130
Morón, 127-128, 171
Morón Reserve, 127
Morro Castle (Los Tres Reyes
    del Morro Castle), 50, 67-68
Morro Castle (in Santiago de
    Cuba), 153-154
murals, 51, 74, 81, 90-91, 139
Museum of Colonial Art, 57-58,
    149
Museum of Indian Civilization,
    138-139
Museum of Natural Sciences
    (Pinar del Rio), 89
Museum of Peasant Traditions,
    107
Museum of Slavery, 125
Museum of the City of Havana,
    49-51, 71
Museum of the Revolution, 60-61
Museum of the Struggle against
    Bandits, 124

Museum of the Underground
    Struggle, 152-153
Museum of Trinitarian Architec-
    ture, 123-124
museums, 105, 107, 123, 149,
    150; archaeological, 73, 108,
    123, 135, 138-139, 146, 164;
    colonial, 57-58, 149; of the
    Cuban revolution, 60-61, 107,
    110, 120, 152-153, 160;
    ethnological, 54-55, 82; of fine
    arts, 57-58, 63; history, 64, 89,
    105, 107, 114, 120, 125, 134-
    135, 138, 152, 154, 160, 164;
    music, 41-42, 112-113; natural
    history, 107, 135, 138; science,
    89, 123
Music Museum, 60

National Aquarium, 77
National Art School, 79
National Ballet of Cuba, 42, 131,
    167-168
National Folklore Group, 42, 75
National Institute of Tourism
    (INTUR), 76
National Library, 74
National Museum of Fine Arts,
    63
National Naval Museum, 120
National Observatory, 68
National Theater, 74
National Workers Federation, 31
National Zoo, 81
natural history. See flora and
    fauna; museums, natural his-
    tory
New Latin American Film
    Festival, 42, 168
newspapers, 43
nuclear power, 39, 119
Nueva Gerona, 94, 96
Nuevitas, 129
Numismatic Museum, 52-53

Obispo street, 53
Obra Pía House, 55
October 10 (national holiday), 4
Old Havana, 45-69
Old Man and the Sea, 82
Old Square, 55-56
opera, 66
Organization of American States, 36
Oriente Province, 140
Orthodox Party, 32
Ortiz, Fernando, 55
Oscar María de Rojas Museum, 107
Our Man in Havana, 63, 64

Pabexpo Pavilion, 167
País, Frank, 33, 153
País, Josué, 153
Palace of the Captains General, 49-51
Palacio de Atesanía Cubana (Palace of Cuban Arts and Crafts), 60
parrandas, 41, 112-113, 114-115
Parroquial Mayor church, 126
passports, 2
Pedrosa family, 57
Peñalver mansion, 57
Perché, 119
Pharmaceutical Museum, 105
Pinar del Río, 89
Pinar del Río Province, 86-92
Pino del Agua, 145
Piracy Museum, 154
pirates, 18, 19, 51, 83-84, 111, 119, 126, 130
Pirates' Coast, 172
Plácido, 22
Plata, 145
Platt Amendment, 30, 94
Playa Girón (Bay of Pigs), 109
Playa Larga, 109
Playitas, 28

Plaza de la Catedral (Cathedral Square), 56-60
Plaza Vieja, 55-56
Portales Cave, 89
Portocarrero, René, 42
Postal Museum, 74
posters, 42, 57
Presidential Palace, 60-61, 62
Primer Palacio, 120
Principal Theater, 131
Protest of Baraguá, 26
Puerta, Capt. Calvo de la, 55
Punta (in Baracoa), 163, 164, 165
Punta del Este Caves, 95
Punta Fortress (San Salvador de La Punta Fortress), 67

queues, 44
Quixote Park, 73

radio, 34, 43
railroad, 14, 15
Rampa, 70-72
Rancho Luna Beach, 120
Real Fuerza Castle, 50, 51
Redonda Lake, 128
Regla, 68-69
Remedios, 41, 111-115
reservations, 14-15
restaurants, 14, 16, 181-183; tips in, 16
Revolutionary Student Directorate, 60, 107
Revolution Square, 73-75
Río Cristal Park, 80
Río Negro Restaurant, 117
roads, 11-12
Romantic Museum, 123
Romero, Juan, 156
Rough Riders, 159
Rueda Restaurant, 79-80
Ruinas Restaurant, 80-81
Rumba Saturday, 42, 75

Sánchez Manduley, Celia, 143
Sánchez Moya, Capt. Francisco, 156, 157
San Carlos Seminary, 59
Sancti Spíritus, 18, 126
Sancti Spíritus Province, 121-126
San Diego de los Baños, 88
San Francisco Convent and Square, 56
San Francisco de Asís Convent, 124
San Francisco de Paula, 82
San Francisco de Sales, 53
San Juan Bautista church, 113
San Juan Hill, 159-160; battle of, 29, 159
San Lorenzo School, 120
San Luis Valley, 125
Santa Clara, 109-111; battle of, 34, 110
Santa Clara Convent, 55
Santa Ifigenia Cemetery, 153
Santa Iglesia Cathedral, 131
Santa Isabel Hotel, 52
Santa Lucía Beach, 132, 172
Santamaría, Haydée, 33
Santa María del Mar Beach, 83, 84
Santería, 21
Santísima Trinidad church, 123
Santísima Virgen de Regla Church, 69
Santiago de Cuba, 13, 14, 146-155, 168
Santiago de Cuba Province, 146-151
Santo Angel Custodio Church, 61, 62
Santovenia, Count de, 52
Sauto Theater, 104-105
scuba diving, 79, 84, 85, 92, 95, 103, 128, 137, 161, 172
Sevilla Hotel, 63
Siboney Indians, 110
Sierra del Escambray, See Escambray Mountains

Sierra de los Organos Mountains, 86, 90
Sierra del Rosario Mountains, 86
Sierra Maestra Mountains, 10, 40, 146; guerrillas in, 33, 143, 145
Sierra Maestra National Park, 145
Sigua Beach, 161
slavery, 18, 21-22, 104, 123, 125; revolts against, 18, 21, 22, 156, 157
Soroa, 86-87, 170
Soroa, Jean Paul, 87
Soviet Union, 36, 37
Spanish language, 43, 172-173, 174-87
sports, 40-41
Stevenson, Robert Louis, 94
Stone Zoo, 162
study opportunities, 172-173
sugar, 38-39, 104, 126; in colonial period, 20, 21, 23, 25, 26-27, 123, 125, 140; prices of, 23, 31
Sugarmill Valley (San Luis Valley), 125

Tabares, Don Gregorio, 53
Taíno Indians, 17, 110, 138, 139, 164
Tango Circle, 150-151
taxis, 13
telephones, 14-15, 187
television, 43
temperatures, mean, 3-4
Templete, 48, 51-52
Tertulia, 113-114
Tesín, Father Juan de, 124
theater, 42, 52. *See also* Havana, theaters in
time zone (Eastern), 3
tinajones, 130, 131
Toa River, 163, 166
tobacco, 17, 19-20, 90, 91, 91-92
Tomás Terry Theater, 120

Topes de Collantes, 121, 170

Torre y Huerta, Carlos de la, 135

tourism, promotion of, 7-9, 39

TRANSTUR, 12

tranvía, 68-69

Treasure Island, 93-94

Treasure Lake, 107, 108

Trinidad, 18, 122-125, 125

Trópico Beach, 83

Tropicana Nightclub, 71-72

tumba francesa, 151, 152

Turiguanó Isle, 128

Turquino Peak, 10, 143

26th of July Amusement Park, 159-160

26th of July Movement, 148, 152-153

26th of July School, 146, 148

Ubre Blanca, 93

Union of Writers and Artists of Cuba (UNEAC), 150, 150

Union of Young Communists, 38

unions, 37

United States: investment of, in Cuba, 26-27, 31; travel to Cuba from, 2, 3

United States government, 1, 2, 27, 28-30, 31, 32, 36-37, 159 universities, 54, 73, 110, 146, 172-173

University of Havana, 54, 73, 172-173

University of Matanzas, 172-173

University of Oriente, 146

Uvero, 145

Valdés, Gabriel de la Concepción, 22

Varadero, 12, 13-14, 167, 171

Varadero Amphitheater, 103, 168

Varadero Beach, 16, 45, 69, 98-103, 169, 172; hotels at, 99-100

Varadero International Music Festival, 103, 168

Varela, Father Félix, 59, 62

Velázquez, Diego, 17-18, 45, 48, 123, 149

Venceremos Brigade, 143

Vermay, Jean Baptiste, 51

Verraco Beach, 160

Vidal, Leoncio, 110

Viejo y el Mar Apartment-Hotel, 79

Villa Clara Province, 109-117

Villa Paraíso, 79

Villaverde, Cirilo, 59, 61, 62

Viñales, 91

Viñales Valley, 10, 90-91

Virgen de la Caridad del Cobre, 156, 157, 158-159

Virgin of Regla, 69

visas, 1, 2

Vuelta Abajo, 91-92

War of Independence, first, 65, 130, 131, 133, 133-134, 135, 140

War of Independence (1890s), 113-114, 159

Weyler, Capt. Gen. Valeriano, 28

wildlife preserves, 107-109

women, status of, 37, 75, 133-134

Wood, Gen. Leonard, 30, 164

Xanadu (Las Américas mansion), 100-102

yachts, 2

Yayabo River bridge, 126

Yoruba culture, 21, 69, 159

Zanjón Pact, 26

Zapata Peninsula, 107-109, 170

Zayas Bazán, Carmen, 25

zoos, 81, 161, 166

ABOUT THE AUTHOR

Jane McManus, a U.S. journalist, has lived and worked in Cuba for twenty years and is currently the editor of *Cuban Sunshine*, a publication of the National Institute of Tourism. In the two years spent researching and writing *Getting to Know Cuba*, she explored all of the island's provinces and personally visited every place mentioned in the guide.